THE FALL OF
DAVID HALL

William R. Burkett
James Edwin Alexander

Macedon Publishing Co. : Oklahoma City

I. Burkett, William R., 1925--
I. Alexander, James Edwin, 1930--

ISBN 0-929965-17-8

The paper in this book meets the guidelines for permanence and
durability of the Committee on Production Guidelines for Book
Longevity of the Council on Library Resources, Inc.

1 2 3 4 5 6 7 8 9 10

Contents

Preface

Three days after leaving office, Oklahoma Governor David Hall was indicted by a federal grand jury for violations of anti-racketeering statutes. The trial took place a month later and lasted three weeks. He was convicted and served 18 months of a three-year sentence in a federal penitentiary.

The trial of David Hall was a noteworthy chapter in Oklahoma's history. It marked the first time a governor of this state was convicted of criminal acts committed while holding the highest office of public trust. It marked a turning point in increasing the public's expectations for honesty and integrity from its elected officials. And it signaled an increasing role by federal prosecutors in exposing and prosecuting corruption in county and state government.

As the U.S. Attorney who brought those charges and conducted the prosecution, I found myself caught in the center of a political maelstrom that was greater than I ever could have anticipated. I was accused of conspiracy, I was disbarred, I was denounced in the Legislature, and all sorts of threats were made against me, including a congressional investigation.

One never knows why fate serves up some of its adventures or why we are called upon to do some of the things we do. I only know that my pilgrimage began in 1949 when I graduated from the University of Oklahoma Law School and moved to Woodward, Oklahoma, to begin my practice of law. With my wife, Phoebe, and daughter, Bana, we came to a town of 5,000 souls that had recently been devastated by a terrible tornado. The only people we knew there were E. M. Beckley, an abstracter, and two lawyers, Tom Hieronymus and Reuben Sparks. Our sons, Jerry and Jim, and our daughter, Julie, were born there. I could not have picked a better town than Woodward to practice law and raise a family.

In 1958 I was elected Republican County Chairman, and very soon after that a wheat farmer from Billings, Oklahoma--Henry Bellmon--was elected state chairman. Two years later, in 1960, I was one of fourteen Republicans elected to the state House of Representatives. Many of us felt we were elected *in spite* of being Republican, not because of it.

At that time, the Republican Party could not be said to be a force in Oklahoma politics, but Henry Bellmon was soon to change that. He amended the party rules to make all elected Republicans members of the state committee and all floor leaders members of the executive committee. He brought the Republican National Committee to Oklahoma City for a meeting at the Skirvin Hotel, and he saw to it that all Oklahoma Republican legislators had a part in that meeting. All in all, Bellmon worked tirelessly to breathe life into a party that was virtually dead.

Henry Bellmon became Governor in January 1963. In April, at his request, I ran for Republican State Chairman. It was a bitter and divisive fight, probably not worth the lumps Bellmon took, but definitely worth it to me. I was, in effect, the Governor's chief assistant for political affairs, giving me an inside look at state government that few people have the opportunity to see.

Bellmon was elected to the U.S. Senate in 1968 and at his request President Richard Nixon nominated me to become U.S. Attorney for the Western District of Oklahoma.

I became U.S. Attorney in July of 1969. At that time I had six assistants, two of whom, John Green and Givens Adams, I retained from the previous administration. My first selection was John Sparks, an assistant D.A. in Oklahoma City and son of Reuben Sparks, then dean of the county bar in Woodward. Sparks, in turn, helped me recruit Jim Peters from Tishomingo, who had been handling condemnation cases for the state highway department, and Floy Dawson from Paden, an assistant D.A. in Payne County. Then we added Jeff Laird, a former FBI agent and general counsel for the Oklahoma Bar Association, who became my first assistant.

I served as U.S. Attorney for six years. There could not have been a better job anywhere. The work was unfailingly interesting, we were marvelously equipped, and I truly believe that no U.S. Attorney ever had a more capable, congenial staff. Our primary arm was the Federal Bureau of Investigation. We had an ideal relationship with the bureau, and I formed lasting friendships with many of the agents.

O. B. Johnston III, from Tulsa, joined us in 1970, replacing John Sparks who returned to Woodward. Later, Susie Lindley, who had just married George Lindley, law clerk to Circuit Judge Bill Holloway, joined us, along with Susie Pritchett, Jerry Cord Wilson, Drew Neville and Bill Price. John Sparks now practices in Woodward, O. B. in Vinita, and Susie Pritchett is Associate District Judge in Kingfisher, Oklahoma. Floy Dawson transferred to the U.S. Attorney's office in San Francisco and has since retired to Austin, Texas. Susie Lindley is a mother and housewife in Duncan, Oklahoma, where husband George is a District Judge. Wilson, Neville, Price and I all practice law in Oklahoma City. John Green is retired from the U.S. Attorney's office. Jeff Laird retired in 1974 and passed away in 1985. John Sparks died in 1997, Jerry Wilson in 1999.

There never were more than ten of us at one time, so everyone carried a full case load of both civil and criminal cases. I assigned categories to each lawyer, and the investigative agencies that produced our cases knew which of us to present them to.

The U.S. Attorney's office has grown since my tenure to more than thirty lawyers, so my successors have been saddled with a lot more administrative duties which have tended to keep them out of the courtroom. I, on the other hand, got to try as many cases as anyone in the office, and I was able to make sure that I tried the major cases--the David Hall trial, of course, being the biggest.

I have often thought there was a great parallel between David Hall and Richard Nixon. I was a Nixon appointee, and I thought highly of him. When the Watergate issue broke I didn't want to believe it. I theorized that the Watergate break-in was done by

Cubans. I tried to rationalize it in every way because I didn't want to believe that my president could do the things they said he did.

A lot of people felt exactly the same way about David Hall. They didn't want to believe their governor would do the things he was charged with. This was not the side of their governor they wanted to see. Indeed, I am sure many of his supporters, to this day, still believe he was innocent.

When the case was over a group of us went to dinner at Sleepy Hollow restaurant. I proposed a toast: "To the system: It works!"

I truly believe that, and that is why I wanted to write this book. A governor proposed a corrupt scheme and worked hard to carry it out. The scheme failed. It failed because other public servants refused to commit such a betrayal; and the governor and his co-conspirators were convicted and punished because of it.

Winston Churchill said: "Democracy is the worst form of government except all those other forms that have been tried from time to time." The same thing could be said for the American judicial system--it is the worst one possible, except for all others. It is widely misunderstood and therefore mistrusted. The least-understood aspects--the technicalities that govern evidence and the seemingly endless appeals--are all rooted in our devotion to the presumption of innocence, a principle that stands squarely between the innocent and the horror of wrongful imprisonment. It may be hard for laymen to understand, but it is the bedrock of our system of criminal justice.

I certainly do not seek to stop criticism of the legal system, even though much of that criticism is uninformed, fueled by emotion, or poor in taste. Nor do I delude myself into thinking I am going to have a measurable affect on people who have learned to dislike and distrust lawyers. I do believe, however, that lawyers and those who support and believe in the legal system should strive to improve it, and they have an obligation to speak up at every opportunity. This case is an example of the system operating at its best, and is my opportunity to speak up.

William R. Burkett, Lawyer

April, 2000

1

The Awakening

...Monday, January 7, 1974.
Office of United States Attorney.   As United States Attorney
for the Western District of Oklahoma, Bill Burkett had become
used to having lawsuits filed against him. His job was to represent
the United States government in all criminal and civil proceedings
within the district.

These lawsuits were not a personal thing, really. Rather, they
were filed against Mr. Burkett "...as U.S. Attorney." Usually,
such suits came from indigents and folks who didn't know any
better. The court always promptly dismissed them.

William R. Burkett cut a singular figure. Trim, intense, modest,
of medium height, and blessed with infectious good wit, the
48-year-old attorney moved with a quick vitality. His narrow,
chiselled face was topped by a furrowed forehead and thinning
brown hair. He had been county attorney for Woodward County,
Oklahoma, served two terms in the state legislature, and officiated
as state Republican chairman before being appointed U.S.
Attorney in 1969.

This lawsuit was different from those he had seen before. It
was filed by the Governor of the State of Oklahoma, David Hall,
and his wife, Jo Evans Hall, both represented by attorneys Byrne
Bowman and Frank McDivitt. Also named as defendants in the
suit were Gene Carrier, the U.S. Marshal, and Clyde Bickerstaff,
District Director of Internal Revenue.

Burkett was shocked to read that he and Bickerstaff, together with their subordinates and agents, were alleged to be preventing Governor Hall's attorneys from interviewing Dorothy Pike, the governor's former confidential secretary concerning an ongoing tax investigation. The suit further requested the court to enjoin [prohibit] them from "counseling, advising, ordering, instructing or encouraging Dorothy Pike to refuse to talk with plaintiff's attorneys and investigators."

This was Burkett's first awareness of Dorothy Pike. He didn't know who she was,[1] nor was he party to any tax investigation involving David Hall.

Immediately, he got on the phone to Phil Harney, deputy regional counsel for the Internal Revenue Service (IRS) in Oklahoma City. "What in the hell is this all about?"

Harney revealed to him that the IRS had indeed been investigating Hall's tax returns. Normal procedures were being followed, to wit: the investigation was being conducted by the intelligence division of the IRS; if they decided that criminal prosecution was called for, the matter would be referred to the tax division of the Department of Justice; then, if the Department of Justice agreed, the case would be referred to the U.S. Attorney in the district in which the taxpayer lived.

Burkett's office would not receive the case until after the Justice Department had made a decision to prosecute. Accordingly, he had nothing to do with their investigation of David Hall and was only marginally aware of newspaper stories that Hall was being investigated by the IRS. Hence, Hall's allegations that Burkett was a party to any such IRS investigation were simply not true.

Harney further related to Burkett that Dorothy Pike had been the governor's confidential secretary and that she left that office in November 1971, a little more than two years earlier. Apparently, during the period she worked for Governor Hall, Pike's duties required her to handle a large number of illegal financial transactions in behalf of Hall, the propriety of which bothered her greatly. So for her own protection, she made a secret record of these transactions which she kept in a spiral notebook. Dorothy Pike's notebook became a crucial piece of evidence in the IRS's investigatory efforts.

Hall's attorneys had been unable to locate Dorothy Pike in order to interview her. Accordingly, the lawsuit against the IRS and the U.S. Attorney was simply legal gamesmanship; that is, a shot in the dark in an effort to find out what was contained in that potentially incriminating notebook.

They sought to use a rule of civil court procedure known as "discovery," in which each side must reveal to the other the evidence they have. However, the law simply does not allow discovery in a criminal investigation. Moreover, this wasn't even a criminal case yet, inasmuch as no decision had been made to prosecute and no charges had been filed.

Furthermore, no one was hiding Dorothy Pike--certainly not the U.S. Attorney's office. Pike was acting under her own volition. Harney was kind enough to furnish Burkett with a handwritten affidavit that Pike had given IRS agents while at her sister's home in Southwest City, Missouri. In this affidavit, Dorothy Pike stated that no one was preventing her from talking to David Hall, she just didn't want to talk with him.

Capping off matters, federal officers are immune from such a lawsuit as this. People simply cannot sue a federal officer for acts pertaining to his or her official duties. But that was exactly what Hall's attorneys were trying to do, seeking to enjoin Burkett from performing his official duties. Obviously, if such lawsuits *were* allowed, anybody with malicious intent could bring the U.S. Attorney's office to a virtual standstill; federal officers couldn't function if they were having to defend their actions in court all the time.

Burkett filed a motion to dismiss, which he had every right to expect would occur. As a part of the motion, he attached affidavits from the other two defendants as well as himself. He also attached a copy of the affidavit from Dorothy Pike, which was probably a mistake inasmuch as it had the effect of bringing Pike into the case in a manner he had not anticipated.

The case was assigned to Federal Judge Stephen Chandler's court. Chandler agreed to hear the motion to dismiss on January 17. But in somewhat of a surprise, he ordered that it be heard on oral testimony. That struck Burkett as unusual, inasmuch as a hearing on a motion to dismiss usually does not involve any evidence at all. Rather, 99 percent of the time it is an argument of pure law. This case should have been an argument of law because where Dorothy Pike was, what she had, whether they were keeping her from talking to Hall, was irrelevant. One simply cannot sue the U.S. Attorney, the U.S. Marshal, and the District Director of the IRS on that basis.

Even more disconcerting to the parties involved, Judge Chandler also issued an order that they "show cause" why he should not grant a preliminary injunction against them.

...Thursday, January 10, 1974
District Office, Internal Revenue Service.   Now that Burkett was up to his ears in the David Hall matter, he asked the IRS to fill him in on the status of their investigation. Special Agent Jack Querry provided the briefing.

Querry described Dorothy Pike as a fortyish, blond, rather attractive, well-kept, very sophisticated lady. She was solid of character, held strong standards about ethics and public morals, exhibited a lot of stamina, and was not one to compromise her beliefs. She had been employed in one of the state agencies before going to work for David Hall.

Querry said that Hall, after his election in 1970--and even before taking office--had persuaded a number of supporters to continue their financial support of him. Ostensibly, these funds were designated as contributions to his campaign war chest, but in reality they were nothing of the kind. Hall diverted the money to pay the personal living expenses of himself and his wife, Jo Evans Hall, that were not covered by the governor's expense account. This largess provided the governor and his family with such niceties as new dresses for Jo, tennis lessons for the children, vacation trips for the family, and the like. It was a sweet deal!

On average, those payments ran somewhere between $5,000 and $8,000 a month. The Halls' tastes were expensive. Each month, David Hall would give Dorothy Pike a list of bills needing to be paid, and Pike would buy money orders and cashier's checks in exact amounts for each creditor, using cash delivered to her by one or another of Hall's confidants. Unbeknownst to Hall, however, Pike carefully recorded the date, serial numbers, amounts and payees of each payment in a spiral notebook that she prophetically labeled "Notes Made For My Protection."

When newspaper stories about an IRS investigation began coming out in May, 1973, Hall suspected that Dorothy Pike--who no longer worked for him--had not only been talking to the IRS, but that she had also given them something of value. The question was, what? To find out, he hired long-time Oklahoma City private detective Robert O. ("Oklahoma Crude") Cunningham to interview her. Cunningham was a former state legislator and widely-known for his coarse and vulgar language.

Dorothy Pike, however, was nobody's fool. She promptly alerted the IRS agents. They told her to go ahead and meet him, but to do so in a public place; and they wired her with a body microphone with which to record the conversation.

That meeting took place in a restaurant in Tulsa. Pike was not the only person recording the interview, as it turns out. Cunningham, too, had a recorder secreted in his briefcase which he set beside the table. Thus, there evolved the somewhat ludicrous situation of two adversaries secretly taping each other.

...Friday, January 11, 1974

Oklahoma State Capitol.   This was the third anniversary of David Hall's inauguration into office as the twentieth governor of the state of Oklahoma. In the eyes of many people, David Hall was as unlikely a candidate for graft and corruption as one could ever expect to see. A handsome, well-exercised, former Air Force officer, and devoted father of three, he was a hulking man in his early forties with a flowing mane of prematurely white hair and an infectious grin.

Hall graduated Phi Beta Kappa from the University of Oklahoma in 1952 where he was on the President's Honor Roll along with Fred R. Harris, who later became a United States Senator. Following Air Force service as a navigation instructor, Hall attended Harvard Law School for one year on a full scholarship that he won in a national contest, after which he returned to Oklahoma to finish his legal training at the University of Tulsa Law School. He was admitted to the bar by special permission of the Oklahoma Supreme Court during his final semester of law school and received an appointment as assistant county attorney for Tulsa County. In February 1962, a year-and-a-half out of law school, Hall succeeded to the office of Tulsa County attorney, resigning in 1966 to run unsuccessfully for the office of governor.

At the age of 35, "Cannonball David Hall," as he billed himself, lost in the Democratic primary by a mere 10,000 votes out of over 500,000 cast.

Four years later, however, using the slogan "Hall of Oklahoma for All of Oklahoma," he squeaked past Republican governor Dewey Bartlett by the closest vote margin in state history--2,181 votes, less than one vote per precinct. The oath of office was administered January 11, 1971, on the Capitol steps by Chief Justice William A. Berry of the Oklahoma Supreme Court. At Hall's side on that clear, crisp, sunny, 50-degree day stood Jo Hall, a vivacious former airline stewardess and now the state's First Lady. And among the 5,000 or so citizens attending the inaugural was Carl Albert, soon-to-be speaker of the U.S. House of Representatives. By any measure, David Hall's political star was shining brightly and his fortunes never looked better.

Chief Justice Berry returned home that evening to a skeptical mother-in-law, Elizabeth Nichols Cox. She asked, "Did you make him swear to keep his hand out of the public till?"

The judge answered with a simple, "Yes."

§ § §

2

The Game

...Thursday, January 17, 1974
The Courtroom.   The "show cause" hearing began in Judge Chandler's court, combined with the motion to dismiss.

Stephen Chandler, 74, was an irascible character who had been on the federal bench since 1943, a patronage appointee of Senator Elmer Thomas. Chandler's elevation to the bench, however, was delayed some three years after he was first nominated.

The judge was a tall, distinguished-looking gentleman with thinning white hair and a once-rugged build. He had long been eligible to retire at full pay but had resisted all pressures and blandishments to get him off the bench. A smoldering feud between Chandler and some of his fellow judges had lingered for years, and he survived their efforts to strip him of authority to receive new cases.

Chandler lived in perpetual fear for his life, having once told a congressional panel sent to investigate the bitter quarrel that his fellow judges were trying to poison him. For that reason, he wouldn't drink from the courthouse water cooler. Nor would he park his car in the reserved spot in the underground parking lot at the Federal Building, fearing that someone might put a bomb in it. Absurdly, though, he drove a highly recognizable red Cadillac convertible which he regularly parked in the public lot across the street, where it was much more accessible to someone bent on mischief.

Chandler also had a reputation for being in a constant war with the government. For example, Burkett once defended the government in a complaint filed against it in which Chandler gave judgment to the plaintiff. Normally in federal court, the United States has 60 days in which to respond to the complaint. Burkett said, "Judge, we haven't even filed our answer yet." He snapped, "There's nothing you could say in an answer that would make any difference."

Another time, there was a guy named Billy Gene Cook who had come across the country on a murder spree. He was arrested in Oklahoma. A hearing for mental competency was held in Chandler's court. Instead of ruling on Cook's mental competency, however, Chandler ruled him guilty on the spot and sentenced him to the death penalty.

With that kind of judge on the bench, things did not bode well for the U.S. Attorney's office.

Appearing with Burkett were Jeff Laird, first assistant, and three assistant U.S. attorneys--Jim Peters, O. B. Johnston III, and Floy Dawson. Representing the IRS was Assistant Regional Counsel Phil Harney. They soon dubbed themselves "The Oklahoma City Six."

Right away, Chandler said that in order to rule on the motion to dismiss he would have to have an evidentiary hearing. Burkett was aghast at this ruling. The motion to dismiss doesn't require any evidentiary hearing, it's a question of pure law. Chandler may have needed a brief, but he certainly didn't need a hearing to show that these were federal employees and not subject to the lawsuit.

Moreover, Hall was being investigated by the intelligence division of the IRS, which meant that it was a criminal investigation. One cannot find out what their evidence is by filing a civil suit, using civil discovery rules--taking depositions, filing interrogatories, demanding the production of documents, etc.--to interfere with a criminal investigation. But, of course, that's what they were trying to do; they were desperate to find out what it was that Dorothy Pike had given to the IRS.

Burkett couldn't escape the feeling that Chandler was trying his damnedest to help David Hall--and not just David Hall personally, but anyone who had a controversy with the federal government. That would explain why he had ordered the "show cause" hearing. In other words, because Hall's attorneys had asked the court to preliminarily and permanently enjoin federal officers from preventing them from interviewing Dorothy Pike, Judge Chandler ordered the government to "show cause" why an injunction should not be issued.

Byrne Bowman called Burkett to the stand as his first and only witness. Bowman was a suave, well-tailored, erudite man in his sixties who had been around a long time. He loved a good fight. He apparently assumed that the U.S. Attorney's office knew everything about what the IRS was doing and was hiding Dorothy Pike from him. That's what his whole lawsuit was about.

Burkett testified that to his knowledge the U.S. Government had no records belonging to David Hall other than those his attorney had furnished to the IRS. He stated that the IRS was "assisting (Dorothy Pike) in having her whereabouts remain unknown to the extent that they can." He told Bowman that Ms. Pike's sister in Missouri might be able to tell him where she was, but as for himself, he did not know her and did not know where she was.

When Bowman finished his direct examination, Burkett then cross-examined himself. That gave him an opportunity to put into the record some things that Bowman did not ask. He testified that neither he nor anyone at his direction had ever counseled, ordered, instructed or encouraged Dorothy Pike to refuse to talk to Hall, his attorneys, his investigators, or anybody else. He said that was also true of the U.S. Marshal and the IRS. Further, he said the government had even asked Ms. Pike to talk to the governor's people, but she said she didn't want to.

Bowman then asked, "Will the government assist plaintiffs in locating and questioning Dorothy Pike?"

"We will not."

"Why not?"

Burkett answered, "Well now, I'll tell you frankly why I won't do it. Because he [Hall] has filed a verified complaint here that alleges that I've obstructed justice. I take that personally, and I resent it, and I wouldn't lift a finger to help him unless it was a part of my official duties to do so."

With that, both sides rested. Judge Chandler then launched into a long, rambling discussion of the investigative procedures of the government, and he wound up suggesting that the IRS give Hall "copies that they have obtained or information pertaining to his tax matters."

Burkett told Chandler that he could not furnish the taxpayer with discovery materials received from third parties; however, it would not be until later at the district and regional IRS conferences that he would have an opportunity to explain his position.

Chandler pressed Burkett to agree to produce Dorothy Pike or to join Hall in requesting the court to order her to appear. Burkett adamantly refused. Finally, the judge recessed until the next day.

...Friday, January 18, 1974

The Courtroom.   Back in court again, Hall's lawyers introduced an amendment to their original complaint. They added the following:

> Justice will be served, and the plaintiffs afforded their constitutional rights, if the court will issue, or direct the issuance, of a summons to Dorothy Pike to appear before this court at a stated date and time and bring with her all records in her possession concerning all transactions by the plaintiffs during her term of employment with David Hall; and, upon her appearance, authorize and permit the examination of her, and examination, and making copies of, such records, by plaintiffs' counsel and by defendants' counsel.

Incredibly, Chandler agreed with this amendment, ruling:

> This Court, I believe, has the power to require her to give her

deposition, require her to come in here and testify if she's subject to process, to subpoena. If she's not, this Court, I believe, has the power to order her deposition, on your request, to order her deposition to be taken....

Clearly, Chandler was wrong. He did not have the authority to subpoena Dorothy Pike to appear in Oklahoma if she was still in Missouri, nor could he subpoena her to appear outside his district. That could only be done by a court in the district where she was to appear. The Federal Rules of Civil Procedure provide: "A subpoena for attendance at a deposition shall issue from the court for the district in which the deposition is to be taken." The rules further provide that "...a subpoena may be served at any place within the district of the court by which it is issued, or at any place without the district that is within 100 miles of the place of the deposition...."

Despite these rules, Chandler claimed that a section of the federal law gave district courts "jurisdiction of any action in the nature of a *mandamus* to compel any officer or employee of the United States or any agency thereof to perform a duty owed to the plaintiff." Applying that provision to this case, Chandler ordered a subpoena be issued to require Dorothy Pike to appear the following Monday, January 21, in Oklahoma City.

At the same time, Chandler seemed to recognize that the subpoena was probably not enforceable, saying, "She's a free agent... [and] technically I couldn't force her to come at the moment." So again he tried to persuade Burkett to join with Bowman in calling Dorothy Pike in Missouri and urging her to appear in Oklahoma City at eleven o'clock, Monday.

Burkett responded, "Well, Your Honor, if she were going to be questioned only about whether or not she has been sequestered or we've interfered with them talking to her, I wouldn't have any objection to doing that; but I'm not going to request her to come down here and be interviewed about those other matters."

Chandler didn't see it this way. He said, "If she's here for other purposes, she's also here for general purposes." He then suggested the U.S. Marshal call Ms. Pike's sister and tell her that the court had issued two subpoenas for Dorothy Pike, one to appear in Oklahoma City, but if she didn't want to come here then the other subpoena would direct her to "appear for the taking at a deposition at a place that she would pick."

The judge went on to order that his reporter be present at any such deposition and that Byrne Bowman and Burkett also be there.

Convinced that Chandler had exceeded his authority, Burkett requested a written order and ten days to appeal to the Circuit Court of Appeals. Chandler said the subpoena would, of course, be written, but his order was not appealable, and a delay would deny the plaintiffs their rights.

Burkett replied, "Your Honor, may I say I don't want to leave the court with a misimpression. The United States does not care whether Ms. Pike talks to these people or they talk to her. That's one thing. But to assert process against her and bring her into Court where she'll be required to answer questions, we do not agree with that. We do not agree that that is proper in this case."

The court recessed for lunch.

At 2:00 p.m., court was back in session. Assistant U.S. Attorneys Floy Dawson and Jim Peters advised the judge that Dorothy Pike was represented by counsel, Art Ruben of Tulsa. Dawson suggested that it would be proper to contact Ms. Pike through her attorney.

Chandler was visibly upset that the government had not already contacted Ms. Pike directly. He grumbled that calling her lawyer would only delay things. Grudgingly, he decided that the deposition should be fixed for the following Monday, and Dorothy Pike should be advised that she could have her lawyer present if she wished. They also carefully worked out the precise wording of what the marshal should say when he reached Pike on the telephone.

But the effort proved to be anti-climactic. When U.S. Marshal Gene Carrier reached Dorothy Pike's sister, he found that Dorothy was gone and her sister professed not to know where she went.

...Monday, January 21, 1974

The Courtroom.   The actors reassembled in Judge Chandler's court. Assistant U.S. Attorneys Susie Pritchett, John Green and Givens Adams joined Burkett at the counsel table. Judge Chandler was not pleased that they had not been able to reach Dorothy Pike. The judge issued a tongue-lashing.

> I realize that you gentlemen here would know that it would be, to say the least, unethical and also, being lawyers, would realize that to attempt to keep her from appearing would be a violation of the criminal laws of the United States, Section 1503, and Section 2 of Title 18, which provides that it would constitute obstructing and impeding justice, and would be a felony, which would apply not only to anyone doing the obstructing or the impeding but to anyone aiding or abetting, and who would be the same as a principal and that would constitute a felony.

After a rambling monologue, he went on to say:

> The only thing I see, now, is to reissue the order or leave the order out--reissue the order for some other time and place. I don't wish at this time to have her brought in. I'll issue a new subpoena today that when she is located, so we can--and I'm sure the authorities ought to be able to locate her and the Court would have the cooperation of all the government agencies to locate her so that we can serve her with the process of taking her deposition.

Burkett asked, ''Is the Court directing the marshal to serve Ms. Pike wherever she is regardless of whether she is within 100 miles of Oklahoma City?''

''Yes,'' he said. He then recessed until 10:00 the next morning.

Burkett returned directly to his office to prepare a petition asking the Circuit Court of Appeals to prohibit the service of the subpoena. The petition was presented to Circuit Judge William J. Holloway, Jr., who resided in Oklahoma City and was in his chambers at the time.

Judge Holloway disqualified himself, citing "the extent of personal acquaintance with the plaintiff, Governor Hall, and the circumstances that a relative... as reported in the press, has been requested to give information in a related proceeding to the Internal Revenue Service." Nevertheless, Judge Holloway forwarded the petition to the Clerk of the Court in Denver.

...Tuesday, January 22, 1974

The Courtroom.   The attorneys found themselves back in Judge Chandler's court again for what they were beginning to call their "ten o'clock flogging."

Judge Chandler produced a new subpoena, handed it to U.S. Marshal Gene Carrier, and ordered him to serve it. The subpoena directed Dorothy Pike "to appear at the place where this *subpoena duces tecum* ('bring with you') is served twenty-four hours after service thereof... and bring with you all records in your possession concerning all transactions as an employee of David Hall and all copies and memoranda made by you at any time of said transactions."

The judge also handed Carrier a second subpoena ordering Ms. Pike to appear at his courtroom at 10:00 a.m. on January 28, 1974, to testify in this case "and bring with you all records in your possession concerning all transactions by the plaintiffs during your term of employment with David Hall."

He closed the session with a warning that anyone knowing the whereabouts of Dorothy Pike had the legal and ethical duty to advise the marshal.

...Friday, January 25, 1974

Circuit Court of Appeals,   *Denver.* The Circuit Court denied Burkett's motion for a stay of Judge Chandler's subpoena, saying that the motion was "premature and the issue posed not ripe."

...Monday, January 28, 1974

The Courtroom.   Judge Chandler was clearly frustrated. Angrily, he issued a new subpoena for Dorothy Pike, along with an additional order:

> This matter is continued for further hearing until 10 a.m. tomorrow, January 29, 1974, and the Marshal is requested to intensify the search for Ms. Dorothy Pike, and the parties are ordered to assist in the search and she is now ordered to appear at ten o'clock a.m. on January 29, 1974.

Burkett immediately sent a written memorandum to Clyde Bickerstaff and Gene Carrier advising them that he intended to appeal that order, but pending the appeal all parties were bound to comply with it. He further suggested that each party should inquire of their agencies about Ms. Pike's whereabouts and to tell him in writing what they had learned.

Then he provided Judge Chandler's office with a formal notice of appeal.

...Tuesday, January 29, 1974

The Courtroom.   Still no Dorothy Pike. Burkett asked to put Governor Hall's attorney, Byrne Bowman, on the stand, at which time he asked if David Hall or anyone on his behalf had ever made any attempt to talk to Dorothy Pike.

"We did not."

"Have you been prevented from doing so by the defendant?"

Bowman admitted that the government had not prevented them from doing so.

Those admissions did not satisfy Judge Chandler, however. He launched into a rambling lecture:

> The whole tenor of this proceeding is, everybody knows, certainly at this point, to bring her in here to testify or to make herself available to be deposed and her discovery

deposition taken. So, I think this is beside the point. The Court has certainly ordered that whether the plaintiffs requested it or not, but the Court ordered it because it thought the plaintiffs had requested it... So it isn't at this point that the plaintiffs have requested it. It's that the Court had ordered it.

At that point Burkett addressed the Court:

Your Honor, may I respectfully disagree and object to this Court's statement that the purpose of this proceeding is to depose Dorothy Pike. If you will recall, this action was commenced by a complaint the prayer of which Mr. Bowman just read to the Court, which was only to keep us from interfering with their talking to Ms. Pike. Now then, we moved to dismiss because it is our contention that they have no right to use this process to require her to appear or even to ask her to appear.

Next, he challenged the Court's role as a willing accomplice in seeking to obtain Ms. Pike's testimony by devious means:

The Court, using the pretext of the Motion to Dismiss, said, "Well, I have to have Ms. Pike's testimony to pass on that." Well, may I suggest to the Court, that if the Court has to have her deposed in order to find out whether or not it has jurisdiction to have her deposed, then of course my Motion to Dismiss is moot. And if, after listening to her testimony, the Court were to sustain my Motion to Dismiss, then I would have won the battle and lost the war, because my attempts to keep her from being deposed would have been defeated by this maneuver. That, of course, is not fair.

Finally, he pointed out that not only did the Court not have jurisdiction to hand over Ms. Pike, but no allegations had been made that they--Bickerstaff, Carrier and himself--even had a duty to deliver Ms. Pike to Hall.

They have offered not one shred of evidence that anybody has ever kept them from talking to her or that they have even tried to talk to her and been unsuccessful. There has been no evidence in here of that. None, Your Honor, not any at all, not even an affidavit from them to that effect.

The judge took offense at Burkett's use of the word "pretext." Actually, Burkett had not intentionally used the word to characterize the Court's actions, although it may very well have been a Freudian slip.

I was a little surprised, Mr. Burkett, at your statement that the Court was proceeding under a pretext, which is not very complimentary, and many judges would consider it contemptuous. I do not because I think it was a slip of the tongue....

I have ruled that I do have the power which means that having exercised it, I have the duty to order her to either come in and testify or be deposed, and I am surprised at your statement that I'm using the pretext of the law and the rules to do that.

Burkett professed, "Your Honor, if I said 'pretext,' I'm sorry. I obviously didn't mean 'pretext.' I mean...."

Chandler interrupted, "It's in the record! I'm just using that as the grounds to be sure I had the power."

Burkett offered an apology. "May I substitute 'grounds' then because that's what I meant? I'm sorry."

"I took no offense at it," the judge retorted sarcastically. "I'm just calling it to your attention."

Following that barbed exchange, the court recessed until February 1. Chandler renewed his order that the parties assist in the search for Dorothy Pike.

No sooner had Burkett returned to his office, however, when Clyde Bickerstaff called Burkett with information that Dorothy Pike had been located in Arlington, Virginia.[1] Burkett passed this information on to Gene Carrier and set to work preparing another petition to the Circuit Court of Appeals, asking them to prohibit the deposition.

Dorothy Pike was served the subpoena that afternoon in Arlington. When Chandler was notified of this, he issued an order for Burkett to appear in his court at 10:00 the next morning.

...Wednesday, January 30, 1974
Circuit Court of Appeals, Denver.   Bill Burkett did not appear in Chandler's court at the appointed hour. Instead, he flew to Denver to deliver his petition in person to Howard Phillips, Clerk of the Court of Appeals. He paced the halls outside Phillips' office while waiting for the court to act. In such instances, the lawyer filing the petition does not see any member of the court. The court acts solely on the contents of the petition.

Meanwhile, Jeff Laird, Jim Peters and O. B. Johnston III represented Burkett at the ten o'clock meeting in Chandler's office. Peters handed the judge's secretary a copy of the petition that Burkett was, at about that same time, filing in Denver. She took it into Chandler. The Judge did not talk to Peters.

An hour later, the writ came down from the Circuit Court. It ordered that "all future proceedings in the United States District Court... be and are hereby stayed." The order was temporary, but it ordered Chandler to show cause in ten days why it should not be made permanent.

Burkett's team thought they had won. But they underestimated the chicanery of their adversary. Wily old Judge Chandler still had a trick or two up his sleeve. After duly notifying Dorothy Pike that her deposition had been stayed, he then advised the parties that Judge Eubanks had transferred to him a related case that also involved Ms. Pike's testimony. Therefore, since the Circuit's order didn't mention that other case, he, Chandler, took the position that he was free to proceed on it as scheduled. A hearing for this second case was set for February 7, 1974.

Thus, Burkett's "victory" proved to be short-lived.

§ § §

3

The Disbarment

...Thursday, February 7, 1974

The Courtroom.   Judge Chandler began a hearing on the
second of two suits filed by David Hall's lawyers. This suit
alleged that the IRS was about to commence civil and criminal
tax actions against Hall and his wife, and that Dorothy Pike had
important information necessary to the Halls' defense. They asked
the court to "perpetuate" (preserve) the testimony of Dorothy
Pike.

This request was based on a provision of the federal rules that
allowed taking the deposition of a witness in a suit to which the
petitioner expects to be a party, but has not yet been commenced,
where the court finds that the perpetuation may prevent a failure
or delay of justice. That case had initially been assigned to Judge
Luther Eubanks, and now was transferred to Judge Chandler.

Chandler asked Burkett, on the record, what representations he
had made to the Circuit Court in support of the application for a
writ of prohibition on January 30.

As a matter of fact, Burkett hadn't seen or talked to any of the
judges when he was in Denver, and he informed Chandler of that
fact. Chandler was being artful. After 30 years on the bench, he
should have already known that petitioners rarely, if ever, talk to
a circuit judge. The normal procedure is for the clerk to take the
petition in to the chief judge, who then assigns a three-judge panel
to consider it.

Nevertheless, he launched into a long tirade that seemed to
suggest that he had a right to go up there and set the record

straight. He said that he thought Burkett had only gone to Denver to file the appeal from his order. (That was not a true statement, inasmuch as Jim Peters had delivered a copy of the petition to his office at approximately the same time it was filed in Denver.)

Chandler said that if he had known Burkett was going to seek an *ex parte* (one party only appearing) order that he would have gone with him to present his side. He said that he was shocked that he was not given notice...that notice was required "by the rules" and by the Code of Professional Ethics, and also by an agreement he thought he had with the U.S. Attorney's office.

Burkett knew this was a "bunch of bull," because they didn't have any such agreement.

The tirade continued unabated, and all Burkett could do was stand there and take it. Chandler told him that in his opinion Burkett had a duty to tell him he was going to file such a petition "one day before" it was filed. He alleged that the order was obtained "under circumstances that are, at least, very questionable" since he did not have an opportunity to appear before the Circuit and "keep the record straight."

There was more. Chandler said that in his view Burkett had the same duty to tell the marshal of Dorothy Pike's whereabouts before his order of January 28 as he did after it. He said that since it was now clear that Burkett knew how to get her address so quickly, he had not told "the whole truth and nothing but the truth" when he had testified he didn't know where she was.

Judge Chandler ended with an ominous warning, "This matter has taken a serious turn by reason of the failure to disclose Ms. Pike's whereabouts and the failure to give notice that an extraordinary writ would be sought."

That undoubtedly was the worst beating Burkett had ever taken from a judge in all his years as an attorney. It was utterly bizarre. Chandler didn't have his facts straight, yet he was an old enough and wise enough judge that he should have known better.

A fleeting thought crossed Burkett's mind that Chandler might have another trick up his sleeve; however, Burkett had other fires to tend. His office was involved in grand jury investigations and preparing for the trial of State Treasurer Leo Winters on extortion charges, and he really didn't have time to give Chandler's machinations much more thought. That may have been a mistake.

...Tuesday, March 12, 1974
Federal Courthouse. Bill Burkett awoke to a shocker. He opened his morning newspaper to read the screaming headline: "CHANDLER BARS BURKETT, AIDES FROM U.S. COURT."

The story by reporter Mike Hammer appeared under the subhead, *Judge's Action Result of Fuss over Mrs. Pike.* Hammer wrote, "U.S. District Judge Stephen S. Chandler Monday ordered U.S. Attorney William Burkett, four of Burkett's assistants, and an attorney for the Internal Revenue Service disbarred as practicing attorneys before the Federal Court in Oklahoma City.

"Judge Chandler also ordered the six men to appear before him on March 21 to show cause why they should not be cited for civil and criminal contempt for their alleged actions in the lawsuit brought against the federal government by Governor David Hall."[1]

What a way to start the day! Hammer noted, "Burkett could not be contacted immediately for comment." Of course Burkett couldn't be contacted duue to the fact that he didn't know a damn thing about it.

The canny old judge had waited until the court clerk's office was closed for the day on Monday, then slipped the order under the door. He also made sure that the newspapers got copies in time for their Tuesday morning editions.

Disbarred, in addition to Burkett, were Jeff Laird, Jim Peters, O. B. Johnson III, and Floy Dawson--all in the U.S. Attorney's office. Phil Harney, counsel for the IRS, was the sixth man.

Burkett now perceived the purpose of Chandler's browbeating lecture on February 7! The judge had been laying a foundation for his disbarment order.

The whole episode would have been ludicrous if it didn't have such serious consequences. The disbarment, if sustained, could not only have a devastating affect on the attorneys' individual careers, but it would paralyze the work of the U.S. Attorney's office. Among other matters, pre-trial proceedings in the prosecution of Leo Winters were scheduled for a hearing on pending motions on that very day before Judge Wesley Brown, who had been assigned from the Kansas district to try the case.

In his order, Judge Chandler detailed six counts against the attorneys. He argued that Burkett and the other named members of the Bar, in violation of their oaths...

1. Did willfully and corruptly conspire... to conceal the whereabouts of Ms. Dorothy Pike from the United States Marshal and the Court after the Court had admonished them to ascertain and disclose her address... which constitutes obstructing and impeding justice in said action.

2. Did willfully and corruptly aid and abet William R. Burkett in concealing the whereabouts of said Ms. Dorothy Pike.

3. William R. Burkett did testify under oath that neither he nor the Internal Revenue Service nor their employees and agents knew the whereabouts of Ms. Pike when in truth and in fact he knew that he could obtain her address and failed to reveal said fact, which constituted perjury.

4. The fact that William R. Burkett had not told the whole truth was known to Jeff R. Laird, James M. Peters, Floy K. Dawson, O. B. Johnson III and G. Phil Harney and they failed to reveal that fact to the Court which constituted the crime of Misprison of Felony.

5. Did conspire to injure David Hall and Jo Evans Hall in the free exercise and enjoyment of their civil rights and privileges secured to them by the Constitution and laws of the United States in violation of Title 18 U.S.C. 241.

6. The said attorneys did conspire to conceal from the Court an Application for Writ of Prohibition and Mandamus of Appeals for the Tenth Circuit on January 30, 1974....

In addition to the disbarment, Chandler issued an order directing that each of the named attorneys show cause within 10 days why they should not be punished for civil and criminal contempt of court.

Upon reaching his office, Burkett was met by Susie Pritchett, the sole member of the team not disbarred. He joked that the judge's obvious preference for females was all that saved her young legal career.

Judge Chandler was wrong on all counts. First, prior to January 28, the "orders" of Chandler were not orders to assist in locating Ms. Pike, they were no more than requests for cooperative effort. These are not necessary predicates for disbarment or contempt.

Second, it follows from the insufficiency of evidence against Burkett that the insufficiency was even more marked as to his assistants.

Third, there was no evidence that Burkett committed perjury. He had made it clear in his testimony that he did not know the whereabouts of Ms. Pike but acknowledged that the IRS had a contact with her through her sister who lived in Southwest City, Missouri.

Fourth, Chandler's contention that Burkett's assistants were accessories after the fact was tenuous and frivolous.

Fifth, the most that could be said of the accusation that Burkett conspired to injure Governor Hall's free rights was that he and his assistants moved to thwart the use of civil procedures to advance the Halls' interest in avoiding an indictment.

And sixth, there was not any semblance of prejudice which resulted from Burkett's failure to notify Judge Chandler in advance of his petition; and in any event, he was never given access to and had no opportunity to communicate with the judges of the Circuit Court.

Burkett couldn't function very well in his office if he was barred from appearing in federal court. To break the impasse, he immediately placed a telephone call to Judge David Lewis, chief judge of the Tenth Circuit Court of Appeals. He apprised Lewis of Judge Chandler's order. By now, of course, the Circuit was well aware of Chandler's predilection for bizarre actions, so they did not hesitate to issue a stay of the order by telephone.

While this conversation was going on, Chandler's three colleagues on the Western District bench were taking action on their own initiative. Fred Daugherty was in Muskogee, Luther Bohanon was in McAlester, and Luther Eubanks was in Oklahoma City. They got together on the telephone and decided amongst themselves that Judge Eubanks would simply enter an order on behalf of all three judges nullifying Chandler's order. By the time Eubanks got to the court clerk's office, however, the Circuit had already telephoned a stay.

The Circuit set September 12, 1974, to hear the appeal of the order of disbarment.[2] Though it still operated under a cloud, the U.S. Attorney's office was nonetheless free to continue its official duties without further hindrance from Judge Chandler.[3]

...Wednesday, March 13, 1974
The Daily Oklahoman.   Tom Laceki, reporter for the Associated Press, weighed in on the issue. His story, carried in the *Daily Oklahoman,* was headlined, "CHANDLER, BURKETT STRUGGLE SHOULD BE DIFFICULT."[4]

Laceki wrote, "Probably nothing in William Burkett's career has prepared him for the fight he suddenly finds himself embroiled in with U.S. District Court Judge Stephen Chandler.

"Burkett, U.S. Attorney for the Western District of Oklahoma since 1969, is no stranger to hard fights. He has served as the county attorney for Woodward County, was elected twice to the state House of Representatives, then defeated the incumbent to become state Republican chairman.

"But this time Burkett may be fighting to save his career; and he is under attack by a judge who more than once has fought the entire U.S. judiciary to a standstill.

"And Burkett has enraged Chandler by defying his authority."

Laceki described Chandler as a formidable foe, saying, "The

last time Chandler took such a step, he succeeded in getting William O. ("Pat") O'Brien of Oklahoma City disbarred, and the men were locked in a bitter legal battle for 12 years. O'Brien never was readmitted to the Oklahoma bar. The judge said he had billed a false claim for $1 million in a federal bankruptcy case."

He concluded, "The fight with Burkett already has acquired some of the convoluted aspects of some of Chandler's career battles." Then he wound up the story by describing some of Chandler's acrimonious battles with the grand jury and his fellow judges.

...Monday, April 15, 1974
Circuit Court of Appeals, Denver.   Arguments were heard on Burkett's petition to prohibit the deposition of Dorothy Pike. The three-judge panel was comprised of Judges Delmas Hill, Robert H. McWilliams, and William E. Doyle. Burkett argued for the defendants, and Byrne Bowman argued for the Halls. The government won.

The court dismissed the suit and made the preliminary injunction permanent. (On November 7, 1975, the Circuit Court wiped out the disbarments because they were not supported by the evidence. For example, Judge Doyle's opinion repeatedly used the expression, "The dearth of evidence is such....").[5]

Thus ended the sorry saga concerning Judge Stephen Chandler.

§ § §

4

The Grand Jury

The Capitol.   Grand jury proceedings are supposed to be secret. But the Oklahoma City and Tulsa newspapers managed to do a pretty good job of keeping the public aware of what was going on behind closed doors. All spring long, there had been a continual outflow of information about the proceedings of county and federal grand juries investigating kickbacks on various state projects.

On this date, State Attorney General Larry Derryberry called on the legislature to consider impeachment proceedings against Governor David Hall. Derryberry said the three-month investigation he had been conducting since January convinced him that the governor had benefited from kickbacks on state building contracts.

At the same time, the attorney general revealed the filing of three anti-trust suits in federal court against firms that had bid on state construction contracts. He alleged the companies funneled money to Hall by setting extraordinarily high costs in their bids.

Hall immediately denied that he had ever received or solicited a kickback and blasted Derryberry as a "Democrat turncoat, modern-day Quisling and Benedict Arnold" for saying that he had.[1] He even suggested that Derryberry, a potential candidate for governor, should register as a Republican.

Any impeachment proceedings would have to start in the House of Representatives. House Speaker Bill Willis, D-Tahlequah, named a five-member special impeachment inquiry committee to investigate the charges.

...Wednesday, May 15, 1974

State Capitol.   The five-man special committee of the State House of Representatives appointed to investigate the charges against Governor David Hall reported that it had declined to call for the governor's impeachment. Committee chairman Representative Don Davis, R-Lawton, said the committee "had determined there is not sufficient evidence to warrant the institution of formal impeachment proceedings."[2]

It was not a complete whitewash. The House passed a resolution that gave Attorney General Larry Derryberry legislative authority to file and prosecute any charges against any state official, including the governor--authority he felt he presently did not have. The resolution, which passed by a vote of 74 to 15, stated that the committee concurred with Derryberry that "other persons not yet charged may be the subject of criminal action as information is developed in pending criminal cases and discovery proceedings are undertaken."

..January-August, 1974

The Federal Grand Jury.   While the IRS was investigating the tax consequences of David Hall's dealings, Burkett convened a federal grand jury to look into the extortion and bribery aspect of these same dealings. They began hearing witnesses on January 24. Thanks to the spadework already done by district attorneys Buddy Fallis in Tulsa and Curtis Harris in Oklahoma City, it didn't take long to make a case.

On April 25, the newspapers broke a story that Burkett's office had been on top of since January, namely, that David Hall did not even wait until taking office before launching his financial chicanery. Soon after the election he sent his top aide, confidant, and fundraiser--a Tulsa businessman named A.W. ("Sunny")

Jenkins--to New York to solicit contributions in exchange for
bond underwriting contracts from Wall Street brokerage houses.
Jenkins was a colorful, wealthy, sinister-looking guy who liked to
be near the center of power. Actually, Hall used him as little more
than a "bag man," constantly raising money. For example,
Jenkins and Hall formed a group called the Governor's Club that
required $1,000 to be a member, and they never had to account
for that money; most likely, it went to Hall.

Jenkins struck pay dirt with Loeb Rhoades & Company, New
York stock and commodity brokers and underwriters. The first
meeting took place in New York on December 10, 1970--a full
month before the inauguration. Attending that meeting were
Sunny Jenkins, David Hall, and Gene Redden. John Loeb, Jr., and
Maurice Sonnenberg represented the brokerage firm. Hall outlined
his plans for road construction and capitol office building projects,
all of which would require massive amounts of bond financing. In
particular, he mentioned the Cimarron Turnpike which alone
would require $74 million in bond financing. This project would
yield nearly $2 million in fees and expenses to whichever firm did
the underwriting. That was a nice piece of bait to dangle before
them.

Scarcely a week passed when, on December 19, Jenkins set the
hook. He told Loeb and Sonnenberg that Hall's campaign fund
desperately needed $100,000. Sonnenberg told Jenkins that they
could raise $25,000 immediately, and if they got the contract they
could raise some more; Jenkins assumed by this that he meant the
other $75,000.

On December 30, Gene Redden, a friend of Hall who was
going to be in New York anyway, picked up the $25,000 and
delivered it to Jenkins in Tulsa. Hall had his secretary, Gerry
Strain, write letters to Loeb Rhoades partners thanking them for
their "contributions" to his campaign. Hall directed that these
letters be pre-dated to a time before the election.[3]

Sometime later, at a meeting in New Orleans attended by Hall
and Loeb, Hall hit up Mr. Loeb for the other $75,000. This pitch
was made in the presence of a former justice of the Oklahoma

Supreme Court.

When questioned about the matter, Loeb Rhoades partner Donald Cates acknowledged that the firm made the payment, but he did not consider such payment improper. He characterized it as a political contribution; however, he did not know the names of the contributors, the amounts contributed, the specific date of payment, or the name of the committee that received the money.[4]

Southwest Bank.   The more the grand jury dug into David Hall's affairs, the more it began to appear as if Hall operated by the motto, "Something in it for you, something in it for me." Unquestionably, the most fertile seedbed for generating bribes and kickbacks was the construction industry. Not only was this the heyday of road construction in Oklahoma, but the state had also begun a massive Capitol office building program, accelerated the expansion of colleges and universities, and poured money into public schools. In the Capitol complex alone, they were building two new state office buildings, a state library, and an underground tunnel system. Governor Hall was the architect of the largest program of capital spending in the state's history; the cash outlays would enrich many contractors and suppliers; and apparently he felt it only right that he should somehow share in the fruits of their good fortune.

One of the names that surfaced early in the investigation was that of Carl Ballew, a painting contractor from south Oklahoma City. An ambitious, lanky, good-natured man in his late thirties, Ballew was another of those persons who wanted to be next to the seat of power. Hall was ready to take advantage of him. He put his arm around Ballew's shoulder and confided in him that he needed four or five thousand a month for personal and family expenses; naively, Ballew agreed to raise it for him.

This arrangement continued for eight or nine months, although the amounts often ran as high as $7,000 or $8,000. Each month, Ballew met with Dorothy Pike--usually at the Southwest Bank in Capitol Hill--who brought with her a list of that month's bills needing to be paid for Hall.

Apparently, Ballew assumed he would be repaid because he himself didn't have that kind of money. Instead, he would borrow whatever money was needed from his bank, take it in cash, and hand it over to Pike who, in turn, would buy money orders and cashier's checks with which to pay the creditors. It was a dumb arrangement, because it was so easily traceable. Besides, Dorothy Pike kept a record of these transactions.

The Habana Inn.   Ballew also figured prominently in another scheme. In December 1972, David Hall had made arrangements with a Shawnee contractor, E. Allen Cowan, in which Hall guaranteed Cowan's company the contract to build two new office buildings in the State Capitol complex. These were the M.C. Connors and the Oliver Hodge buildings, housing the tax commission and education department, respectively. In return, Hall demanded a payment of $122,000.

The payoff came on December 19. Cowan borrowed the money from the American National Bank in Shawnee, delivered in brand new $20 bills still bound in Federal Reserve wrappers, which he packed neatly into a briefcase. The money-laden briefcase was given to Sunny Jenkins who, in turn, telephoned Carl Ballew and instructed him to pick it up at the Habana Inn on Northwest 39th Street in Oklahoma City.

Ballew, when he got there, became frightened for his own personal safety. So he did what every red-blooded businessman would do--he telephoned his secretary and told her to come pick it up for him. Dutifully, Ballew's secretary came with her husband to the motel, picked up the briefcase, and took it to their home.

Curiosity got the better of the pair, so she and her husband opened the case to see what it carried. Stacks upon stacks of brand new $20 bills, still in their Federal Reserve wrappers, stared back at them. Realizing that everything was not entirely on the up-and-up, they took pictures of the money for their own protection.

The photographs were brought to the attention of the IRS in May of 1973. Special agents Jack Querry and Bill Maynard were working the case. They had the photos blown up to a size that they could read the serial numbers on the Federal Reserve wrappers. Then, by contacting the Federal Reserve Bank, they were able to trace those notes to the Shawnee bank from whence they came.

Querry and Maynard drove to Shawnee to talk to the bank officer who had signed the receipt for the money. The bank officer became extremely agitated and insisted, "I know *nothing* about that. You'll have to talk to our president."

The bank's president, Harbour Lampl, gave his version of the events. According to him, Cowan insisted he needed the money in cash because he frequently attended heavy equipment sales in which on-the-spot cash payment was often the means to closing the sale.

When the agents talked to Cowan, however, he offered yet a different version of the story. He told Querry that he had borrowed the money for only a short while--actually keeping it at his home--and then he took the money back to the bank and paid off the note a few days later with the exact same bills. The reason for the rapid repayment, he said, was to enhance his credit rating with the bank.

Of course, Cowan's explanation didn't hold water, and Querry and Maynard knew it. Their proof lay in the pictures taken at the home of Carl Ballew's secretary. Actually, the money that Cowan used to repay his debt came from the state of Oklahoma by means of inflated payments. Cowan had instructed his sub-contractors to submit padded invoices on their projects, the sub-contractors then returned the overpayments to him in cash, and it was this cash that he used to repay the note at the bank.

The trail led directly from the Shawnee contractor to Carl Ballew. Confronted with his complicity in the matter, Ballew readily agreed to talk in return for immunity from prosecution. It was he that led the agents to Dorothy Pike and her valuable spiral notebook.

State Board of Affairs.   Another casualty of the Hall regime
was Lynn D. ("Buddy") Hall--no relation to David Hall-
-Chairman of the State Board of Affairs, the agency that handled
all state office buildings and purchasing services and was
responsible for administering millions of dollars in contracts.
Back on January 25, he had been called before a state grand jury
to talk about some money that various contractors said they had
been paying him.

Buddy Hall refused to testify, claiming his Fifth Amendment
rights under the Constitution--as he had previously before a state
grand jury. Governor Hall professed to be "shocked" by Buddy's
"taking the Fifth," and he fired him immediately. The governor's
press secretary, Ed Hardy, issued a statement that, in light of what
was already known about David Hall's own record, seemed a bit
hypocritical, to wit:

> The governor had made it, I think, quite clear to anyone who
> is an employee of state government, by virtue of his position
> on the Buddy Hall matter and his statements at that time, that
> employees of the public ought not be taking the Fifth
> Amendment. That's just not a proper posture, and it's really
> not an acceptable posture.

...July-August, 1974

The Grand Jury.   As kind of a side issue, the grand jury also
looked into a $35,000 contribution made to Hall's 1970 campaign
by State Examiner and Inspector John M. Rogers from his own
campaign war chest. Rogers' last campaign did not draw an
opposing candidate, which meant that he had a substantial sum of
money left over which he couldn't use. Being a good Democrat,
he passed some of it on to his party's gubernatorial candidate.

There was nothing illegal about Rogers' action. However, for
some dumb reason Ollie Gresham, a Tulsa attorney, and two
young attorneys in his office who worked in Hall's campaign,
decided they ought to "launder" that money. So, they set up a
scam whereby checks written from Rogers' campaign account

would flow through willing accomplices into the Hall war chest. Now, lying about it to a grand jury was illegal.

Gresham disclaimed any knowledge of the scheme and was indicted for perjury, a charge to which he ultimately pled guilty.

...Tuesday, August 27, 1974

The Election Commission.   In his bid to become the state's first two-term governor, David Hall lost badly in the Democratic primary, coming in a poor third. He drew only 169,290 votes--a mere 27 percent of the votes cast--compared with Clem McSpadden's 238,534 and David Boren's 225,321. Boren, a young state representative from Seminole, went on to win both the Democratic runoff and the general election.

Despite having the political endorsement of the state AFL-CIO and the support of many educators, Hall was unable to overcome the adverse publicity surrounding his administration. For all practical purposes, his political career was over when the grand jury testimony came out about the kickbacks, and he lost all credibility with his abortive lawsuits against Burkett and an ill-conceived suit against Southwestern Bell alleging his telephone was bugged.

Still, Hall put up a brave front and seemed to have lost little of the charm for which he was famous. He began making plans for what he would do upon leaving office. For example, he talked about possibly running for the U.S. Senate, and he also confided in several friends that he had a "piece of the action" in a resort development project in Palo Mesa, California, that he might pursue.

...Thursday, September 5, 1974

The Grand Jury Room.   John M. Rogers and John Rogers, father and son, were called to appear before the grand jury in connection with the financial contribution made to Hall's 1970 campaign. Both took the Fifth.

...Friday, September 6, 1974

The Grand Jury Room.   Governor Hall, waving to a crowd of well-wishers, reporters, and the just plain curious, strode jauntily up the walk of the Federal Courthouse in Oklahoma City. He was on his way to provide testimony before the federal grand jury. Accompanying the governor were his press secretary, Ed Hardy, his tax attorney, Frank McDivitt, and defense attorney, D. C. Thomas.

To see him, one would have thought he was still on the campaign trail. He called out "Hi!" and "How're ya doing?" to people in the hallway as he went along. At one point, he even bent down and shook a small boy's hand before entering the elevator that whisked him to the fourth floor.

The reporters waited. Some were smoking cigarettes, some writing in their pads, some engaged in idle chit-chat. All wondered what was going on behind the closed doors.

Hall was in there little more than five minutes. He emerged grim-faced and sullen. Reporters clustered around him as he strode angrily toward the door and his waiting limousine. Again and again they shouted out, "Governor, did you take the Fifth?"

"No comment! No comment!" was his only reply as he barged unceremoniously through the crowd, head down, never looking up to make eye contact with any of the pursuing inquisitors.

After chasing the governor out of the building, the reporters returned to question Bill Burkett. "Did Governor Hall take the Fifth Amendment?" they wanted to know.

Burkett played coy, saying he was not being permitted to tell what went on in the grand jury room.

Instead, he gestured with the thick stack of documents in his hand; and acting like the cat that just swallowed the canary, he posed a question to the reporters, "What do you think?"

In case they failed to get the point, he added, "Look how long he was in there."

It seemed ironic, and perhaps even deliciously deserved, that the man who earlier had so sanctimoniously castigated Buddy Hall for taking refuge in the Fifth Amendment should now find himself doing the exact same thing. Whatever credibility and whatever political future the governor may have had left, it was now gone. For in the eyes of the media and the general public, his refusal to answer questions before the grand jury implied a presumption of guilt.

...Monday, September 9, 1974
The Department of Justice, Washington, D.C. By this time, Burkett figured they had a strong case against Hall and was ready to ask for an indictment. Five contractors were lined up to testify, each of whom had paid cash to Hall to get state contracts--including Allen Cowan of Shawnee.

The Justice Department was ready to approve the indictment on bribery and extortion, and Burkett could have gone to trial on that basis. However, he wanted to strengthen the case by adding some counts on tax evasion, believing they would have a better chance of getting a conviction. (Earlier, he felt he'd made a mistake in the Leo Winters case by not including tax charges, and they ended up getting a hung jury. Winters was acquitted in a second trial.) The IRS was in full agreement with their adding these charges to the Hall indictment; however, it would have to be approved by the tax division of the Justice Department.

Three federal officers went to Washington, DC, to plead their case for adding tax charges--Burkett, Phil Harney, and Larry Naiser, chief of the Intelligence Division of the Oklahoma City office of the IRS. They met with the head of the tax division of the Department of Justice, Assistant Attorney General Scott Crampton.

Mr. Crampton listened sympathetically to their arguments, but he demurred in making a decision about adding the tax counts. Why? No reason given. Burkett was inclined to believe that Crampton was skittish about prosecuting politicians.

The case against Hall was put on temporary hold while awaiting the Justice Department's determination.

§ § §

5

The Chase

...Tuesday, December 3, 1974
The State Capital.   Something happened that changed the
entire course of the investigation. Governor David Hall made a
telephone call to Secretary of State John Rogers.

"What happened to that investment deal that was suggested by
the people from Texas?" Hall asked.

"We didn't pay any attention to it," Rogers replied.

Hall sounded annoyed. "John, that's no ordinary deal. Come up
to the Blue Room and meet me there."

Rogers, age 46 and the son of John M. Rogers, State Auditor
and Inspector, was a smiling, mustachioed, stocky, raven-haired
member of a powerful political family and often mentioned as a
likely candidate for the next U.S. Congressional race which would
be coming up in 1976. One never doubted his political ambition.

The Blue Room is a ceremonial room that adjoins the
governor's suite on the second floor. Hall often used it as a
private conference room when he wanted to carry on a
confidential conversation out of ear-shot from his office staff.

Dutifully, Rogers walked up from his first-floor office to meet
with the governor. Hall got right to the point. "Look, there's
$50,000 in this thing. If we can get it done, I'll split it with you."

The "deal" that Hall was referring to was a proposal from W.
W. ("Doc") Taylor, a Texas businessman and financier, to
borrow $10 million[1] from the state retirement fund which he,

Taylor, would in turn lend out to minority and disadvantaged small business enterprises. The program ran under the auspices of the Small Business Administration and was, in some fashion, guaranteed by the U.S. government. Taylor had already peddled the idea to several other states besides Oklahoma, including Texas, but met with no success.

Initially, Taylor had made the presentation to Max Stange, director of the Oklahoma Public Employees Retirement System (OPERS), on November 8--an appointment made by the governor's office. Stange flatly told the Texan, "Listen, I run the office, but I don't have anything to do with investments. You'll have to talk with the board, and the board chairman is John Rogers, Secretary of State." Feeling rebuffed, Taylor retreated to the governor's office where a secretary made an appointment for Taylor to see Rogers later that afternoon. On the following Wednesday, November 13, Rogers pitched Taylor's proposal to the investment committee, but the members were totally unimpressed. They didn't know Taylor, didn't know anything about him, and they literally pitched his proposal in the trash basket.

But Governor Hall was not ready to let the project die. Unbeknownst to Rogers, Hall had stopped off at Meacham Field in Fort Worth in the state airplane during a December 2 trip to Houston, at which time he held a private meeting with Taylor. Taylor's primary business was done through a company named Southwest Mortgage, but he also had a company named Guaranty Investment Corporation. The latter company was the vehicle through which he hoped to do business with Oklahoma. Hall wanted to talk about venture financing for his resort development project at Palo Mesa, California, and Taylor wanted to talk about his loan project with the Public Employees Retirement System in Oklahoma. Attending the meeting also was R. Kevin Mooney, a law school classmate of Hall's who worked in the Taylor organization.

As Hall and Mooney were walking back out to the airplane together, Hall said to him, "This is a good deal and I'll help him with it, but it's worth one point ($100,000).[2] I want it paid to me over four years after I leave office; and I'll split it with you.''

The next day, Mooney reported back to Hall, ''Taylor said 'Okay.' He said he's used to paying finder's fees.''

This was the genesis of Hall's crass offer to John Rogers. Rogers was aghast and didn't want any part of it, but he didn't say so. He left the Blue Room a shaken man. He went by a circuitous route to the attorney general's office so as to avoid Hall seeing him go there.

Attorney General Larry Derryberry was not in his office. Rogers paced the floor nervously. ''I've *got* to see him,'' he pled. The secretary promised, ''I'll have him call you as soon as he gets in.''

...Wednesday, December 4, 1974
The State Capital.   Derryberry returned John Rogers's call. Rogers told the attorney general about the bribe offer, and he insisted that he and Derryberry--or at least some state people--needed to resolve the matter. ''If you could wire me for sound,'' he offered hopefully, ''I can get him in a conversation and I can prove this thing.''

Derryberry immediately took up the matter with Tom Puckett, chief assistant at the Oklahoma State Bureau of Investigation (OSBI). The OSBI was the state's chief investigative arm. Puckett and Derryberry agreed that the state had a serious situation on its hands, one that ought to be investigated. However, they were faced with a problem. The OSBI was directly under the governor. So they also agreed the OSBI was probably not the agency to carry out the investigation.

Derryberry's next alternative was to bring in the FBI. He asked Ted Rosack, Special Agent in Charge, if the FBI could loan him some agents. ''We don't do that,'' Rosack replied.

''Well, could you loan me some equipment?''

''No, we don't loan equipment either,'' Rosack said. ''If we're in on a case, we're in charge.'' In other words, for the FBI to get involved, it has to run the show.

That was okay with Derryberry. Prosecuting a sitting governor was a hot potato that he'd just as soon not handle.

...*Monday, December 9, 1974*
Lawton, Oklahoma. Bill Burkett was in Lawton, Oklahoma, trying a case that ended shortly after lunch. A call came in from Larry Derryberry, catching him just as he was leaving the courthouse. The first thing he said was, "Is this telephone all right?" Burkett replied, "Larry, I always assume all telephones are all right because it's just too much trouble otherwise."

Derryberry's speech was guarded. "I don't know if we can prove it or not but John Rogers swears that David Hall offered him a bribe, and if we can get him wired up for sound, he thinks he can prove it."

Burkett told him, "Well I'm just now leaving Lawton. Meet me at Ted Rosack's office."

The drive back to Oklahoma City took about two hours. It was nearly 4:00 p.m. by the time Burkett got to the FBI office at Fifty Penn Place. Already there were Rosack; Paul Baresel, a longtime, highly respected, and very, very good FBI agent who would be the case agent in this matter; Jack DeWitt, who was the FBI's electronics expert; Larry Derryberry; and John Rogers.

After discussing the situation for a few minutes, Ted Rosack called Washington and got permission to use electronic materials- -tape recorders and the like. The rule is that it's legal to tape a conversation so long as you have permission of one of the parties to the conversation; you don't need a court order to do it. On the other hand, if they were going to tape a conversation between two people who didn't know they were being recorded and didn't give their consent, that would be a "wire tap," and to do that they would have had to show probable cause and get a warrant. But no warrant was needed here inasmuch as they had John Rogers' consent. To make sure, they had Rogers sign a consent statement.

They rehearsed their procedures. A plan was devised whereby Rogers, whenever he was going to have a conversation with David Hall, would call the FBI beforehand and they would come to his office to put a recorder in the small of his back and cover it with tape, then start it running. To assure himself of the quickest route to the State Capitol where Rogers' office was located, Agent Jack Dewitt practiced driving from the FBI office to the state Capitol.

Because nothing is foolproof, the agents devised a backup procedure to cope with "Murphy's Law," namely, *Whatever can go wrong, will go wrong.* For example, a conversation with the governor might run longer than the tape reel, thus causing them to miss recording some really incriminating statements; or perhaps the tape might jam in the machine. So, to get around these problems, they also affixed a small radio transmitter to Rogers' chest which transmitted to an FBI agent seated in a car outside the Capitol. This device had a range of 2 or 3 city blocks.

...Thursday, December 12, 1974
State Capitol.   Taping of conversations began when Kevin Mooney came to Oklahoma City to talk with John Rogers about the proposed deal.

Mooney was something of an enigma to the investigators, and they didn't know a whole lot about him. He was a nice-looking fellow, 44 years old, law-school classmate of David Hall, lived in Texas, but didn't practice law. Apparently, he worked with Doc Taylor and hoped to make some money off Taylor's activities. In this deal, he appeared to be the go-between.

Rogers took Mooney into the attorney general's office and introduced him to First Assistant Attorney General Marvin Emerson and to Mike Martin, a bond expert. The pretext for this meeting was that the attorney general's office was going to have to examine this plan and give an opinion on it.

In this recorded conversation, Mooney acknowledged that he was the contact man between Taylor and Hall. Rogers mentioned the $50,000. Mooney said that he knew about that. They discussed the interest rate, and Mooney said that if Rogers could get this deal approved at 8 percent interest, "we would really be cutting a fat hog."

Mooney brought with him the draft of a letter that John Rogers, or someone representing the retirement fund, was supposed to write to Doc Taylor on state letterhead agreeing to this deal. Rogers had it typed up on his office letterhead, but he didn't sign it.

Also, there was an offering circular from Taylor that had been delivered to the First National Bank, the fund's investment advisor. Rogers made a trip down to the bank to pick up the circular, which he then gave to the attorney general's office.

The tape ran out before the conversation ended, but Rogers didn't think it missed anything of consequence.

...Tuesday, December 17, 1974

The Home of John Rogers.   Rogers telephoned Kevin Mooney in Dallas and told him that the attorney general's office had some questions. Mooney replied that he and Taylor would fly into Oklahoma City on the 18th and meet with the attorney general and his staff.

...Wednesday, December 18, 1974

Office of the Secretary of State.   Mooney and Taylor talked to John Rogers in his office. This was a very productive conversation. Rogers proved to be a great actor and improviser. In fact, he seemed to really be enjoying his role.

For example, he asked Taylor, "Would it be worth any more to you if I could get it (the loan) through at 8 percent?" Taylor agreed to pay an additional 1/8th of a point, another $12,500.

Now, the investigators had not suggested anything like that to Rogers. He just winged it. He acted just brash enough that they never doubted he was a con man who would take a bribe, but not so brash as to cast suspicion on his acting.

In the course of the conversation about payment, Taylor told Rogers, "Any payment we make we would have to show in the prospectus, so what we have to do is to pay you in some other way, like hire you to make a feasibility study on a project that isn't going to go anywhere--because there's no following of the funds in that kind of a deal." Rogers countered, "Well I've got a building that's mortgaged and it's vacant, maybe you could help me find a tenant for that." The matter was left open-ended.

That evening, Rogers telephoned David Hall, who was in California, and brought him up to date. He said the papers were being reviewed by the attorney general.

They discussed when to call a meeting of the pension fund trustees. Hall agreed to call his people--meaning, the ones that he would contact to encourage to vote for this proposition--and he would call Rogers back the next morning with a report.

Rogers then told him about the extra 1/8th point he finagled for getting the loan through at 8 percent. Hall seemed pleased with that.

Unfortunately, the sound quality of this recording was very poor and parts of the conversation were missed. However, there was enough good stuff on tape to confirm there was going to be a payoff and Rogers would participate in it.

...Thursday, December 19, 1974
Office of Secretary of State.   The next day Rogers got a call from Hall in California in which Hall reported that he had talked to Dick Ward, director of the state highway department and a trustee of the pension fund, but Hall said he still needed to talk to two more trustees. About 30 minutes later, Hall was on the phone again to Rogers to say he still hadn't been able to reach the other two trustees.

Around mid-afternoon Rogers got a third call from Hall. This time, Hall said he had now lined up his trustees, and he asked Rogers to call a meeting of the board for 10:00 a.m. on the next day and put the deal through.

Rogers wanted to know which trustee would make the appropriate motions in the meeting. Hall told Rogers that he would have to line up someone and to handle it himself.

...Friday, December 20, 1974
The State Capitol.   The board meeting was held at 10:00 a.m. to consider Taylor's proposal. Taylor was not present. He had

called earlier in the morning to say that he couldn't get a plane up from Dallas until around 11:45.

Members of the board of trustees were Rogers, chairman; Jim Cook, Commissioner of Charities and Corrections; Leo Winters, State Treasurer; L. P. Williams, State Commissioner of Labor; J. O. Spiller, Director of State Finance; Richard A. Ward, State Highway Director; and J. L. Merrill, a member of the State Tax Commission.

Voting in favor of the proposal were Rogers and L.P. Williams; J.O. Spiller and J.L. Merrill voted against it; and Dick Ward--whom the governor thought he had lined up--abstained. Leo Winters did not attend. Thus, the item did not pass.

Taylor arrived about 12:15, and the FBI placed him under surveillance from the time he got off the plane and drove into Oklahoma City. Rogers briefed Taylor on the morning meeting. That was caught on tape.

Later, when John Rogers briefed Burkett on the meeting, he reported that J. O. Spiller said, "This is crazy... a lame duck governor trying to put through a $10 million deal in the waning days of his administration... we don't know anything about this... I wouldn't vote for that for anything!" That information caused Burkett a bit of anxiety, because Spiller had an extremely logical mind and was pretty outspoken.

Nevertheless, Burkett was sure there would be other board meetings on this--that Hall would not let the matter die--and he was afraid Spiller's outspokenness might wreck the investigation. He was making a lot of sense and probably would have persuaded the other board members. On the other hand, Burkett couldn't ask Spiller to vote in favor of the proposal without giving him more information than he wanted to give. So, what he did was call him up and, without telling him what was going on, simply asked him as a personal favor not to attend any more meetings. Spiller seemed happy to oblige.

...Sunday, December 22, 1974

The Home of John Rogers.   Hall telephoned Rogers. This conversation was recorded on tape. Rogers reported on the meeting of the 20th. Hall was displeased; he asked why the deal was presented at 8 percent. Rogers said he did it so that the cut for them would be higher.

Hall instructed Rogers to call another board meeting and present the deal at 8-1/4 percent. He said, "Now, your excuse for recall of the meeting was that now they will go for 8-1/4 percent."

Rogers reminded Hall that he (Rogers) and Kevin Mooney had an appointment with Hall the next day. Hall said to forget about that appointment, "I don't want Mooney showing up in my office the same day you all are going to vote on that."

That evening, Mooney called Rogers at Rogers' home--also recorded on tape. Mooney said he was calling because Hall had asked him to, that he (Mooney), had "twisted Hall's arm" to call another meeting of trustees and re-present the matter. Mooney said he would come up the next day.

Later on in the evening, Mooney phoned again to advise Rogers that he and Taylor would be flying in the next morning.

...Monday, December 23, 1974

The Office of the Secretary of State.   At 8:00 a.m., Rogers took a call from David Hall in which the governor asked him to hold off calling a meeting of the trustees since he had not yet talked to his "man." Hall called Rogers back at 10:00 and gave him the go-ahead to call the meeting for 3:00 that afternoon.

Mooney and Taylor came into Will Rogers World Airport about 11:45. Their arrival was observed by FBI agents sitting in the outer lobby, making out as if they were ordinary citizens. Rogers briefed them on plans for the upcoming meeting.

Rogers convened the meeting promptly at 3:00 p.m. with Dick Ward, L. P. Williams, Jim Cook, and J. L. Merrill all being present. A motion was introduced to have the fund make the investment as revised to 8-1/4 percent interest. The motion failed to pass.

Rogers recessed the meeting and called Hall to report the committee's action. Hall told him to try for a third time, but this time amend the motion to approve the investment "...if and when approved by the attorney general and the First National Bank." Hall reasoned that it might relieve the reservations of the trustees if the ultimate decision could be passed down the line.

The third time was a charm. The motion passed with Ward, Rogers and Williams voting *for*, Cook abstaining, and Merrill voting against.

After the meeting adjourned, Rogers, Taylor and Mooney met again in Rogers' office to discuss the outcome. Taylor thought he had a 50-50 chance to sell the deal to the people at First National Bank. Mooney was more pessimistic; he did not think the bank would approve. Taylor remarked, "Well, Hall is not going to retire to California if the deal does not go through!" The obvious implications were that Hall was going to use the powers of his office to persuade the bank to accept the plan and that he had a financial interest in the outcome.

Rogers asked them when he was going to see some money. Taylor and Mooney told him they were willing to bring half of the payoff amount when the deal was approved by everyone up and down the line, and the second half when the first check was drawn. Half of the payoff amount, the investigators assumed, would be $31,250--half of $62,500.

Rogers then called Hall in California to report the results of the board meeting. Rogers offered his opinion that the bank would write a letter the next day turning down the proposal. He asked the governor what influence he had on the bank. Hall said he would handle this one differently and go to "Leo" and get him to intercede in this matter. ("Leo" was State Treasurer Leo Winters who, by virtue of his power to control state deposits, had tremendous stroke with the banks.)[3] Hall also asked Rogers to go down to First National Bank and see what he could do.

Hall called Rogers back that evening at his home and said he couldn't get ahold of Leo Winters. He suggested Taylor should go to the bank and sell the deal himself and that Rogers should tell the bank that if they didn't go along with the deal the state would move its account out of that bank.

A little while later, Rogers got another call. This one was from Kevin Mooney in Dallas. Mooney said he would be driving through Oklahoma City on his way to Tulsa on the 24th for the Christmas holidays, and he would like to pick up the preliminary commitment letter from the bank on his way.

...Tuesday, December 24, 1974
The Office of U.S. Attorney.   John Rogers was obviously enjoying his new-found role as an undercover man. A little too much, perhaps.

Bill Burkett was in the midst of the Christmas party at the U.S. Attorney's office when he took an urgent call from Paul Baresel, the FBI agent on the case.

Baresel was agitated. He said that John Rogers was down at First National Bank talking to two young officers in the trust department. In a clumsy attempt to get them to go along with the deal, Rogers told them that he was working with the FBI and the government investigating David Hall, and he needed to get a letter approving this deal...right now!

They, quite naturally, were skeptical. And when they wouldn't give him the letter he wanted, Rogers called Baresel and asked him to back him up. Baresel told him, "John get those two young fellows and meet me on the street. I will pick you up!"

Baresel brought Rogers and the two bank officers to Burkett's office. As yet, Burkett had not told any of his assistants about the investigation. It was a ticklish situation; yet even though a Christmas party was still going on down the hall, he ushered the group into his private office. Burkett explained to these two young bank officers that there was an investigation going on, that he did not want them to do anything, but when their boss, William O. ("Bill") Alexander, got back from Christmas holiday, he would talk to him about it.

Although they managed to avert a catastrophe, the investigators were beginning to see that John Rogers could become a problem--all because of his loose tongue.

...Thursday, December 26, 1974

The State Capitol.   Rogers put in a call to the governor's office, thinking Hall would be back from his vacation. He wasn't; Hall was in Park City, Utah, skiing. Rogers left word for the governor to call him back.

When Hall later telephoned from the resort in Utah, Rogers briefed him about the results of his contact with the bank--in essence, no letter of recommendation. Hall, for his part, reported that he had talked to Leo Winters, and Leo said he did not want to pressure the bank.

Things appeared to be at a standstill. Then, Hall came up with a last-ditch suggestion, namely, that Rogers call another board meeting and have the trustees vote to make the investment without the bank's recommendation.

Rogers, ever the actor, tried to get Hall to talk about their payoff arrangements. He said, "I don't want those guys coming up here without the money."

Hall replied sternly, "Don't talk about that on the telephone!"

When Burkett heard the tape of Hall saying that, he nearly jumped out of his skin. That was probably the most incriminating thing that he had said in any of the recorded conversations up to that point. He went on to say that he would be back in Oklahoma City on the 31st, and then he would tell Rogers exactly how he wanted things handled.

...Friday, December 27, 1974

First National Bank.   Doc Taylor came to Oklahoma City for an appointment with Bill Alexander, trust officer at First National Bank.

Alexander had already been briefed on the situation. Burkett told him that the U.S. Attorney's office did not want to get the bank involved in anything illegal or unethical. Naturally, Alexander was concerned about the bank's potential liability in this matter. He agreed that while, on the one hand, he would not issue a letter of approval, on the other hand, he would do nothing to discourage Taylor from thinking such a letter might be forthcoming.

So that's exactly what happened. Alexander received Taylor warmly and in such a manner that he caused Taylor to conclude that the bank *would* approve it. Burkett learned this in a roundabout way when Mooney later called Rogers to say that Taylor thought everything was going to be okay.

Something happened that night that nearly blew the whole deal out of the water, and that something was again John Rogers and his loose tongue. A fellow named Robert Sanders, a former Oklahoman now living in Florida, came through the state. He came by the Capitol to see old friends, including John Rogers. Incredibly, Rogers confided to him the whole story about Doc Taylor, the governor, the $50,000 bribe, how he was working with the FBI, and all that good stuff.

Why did Rogers do that? Who knows. One reason possibly was that he was so "full of himself" that he just *had* to tell somebody. Maybe he was just trying to impress his friend with his own importance, believing that Sanders would hold it in confidence. Whatever the reason, it was not a very smart thing to do.

Over dinner that evening, Sanders got to thinking about what Rogers had told him. It concerned him. So he called Gerry Strain, the governor's secretary. "I need to talk to the governor," he said. "Where is he?" Strain said she would contact Hall, then in Utah, and have him get in touch with Sanders.

Sanders got a call from Hall. The conversation went something like this: "David, if I said to you 'John Rogers,' 'Doc Taylor,' and '$50,000,' would that mean anything to you?"

Hall hedged a bit. "Well...., I know about the deal with Doc Taylor... the proposal he's made to the state is good. Why?"

"Well, John Rogers says he's setting you up on this deal, and he's going to get you."

...Monday, December 30, 1974
Home of Special Agent Paul Baresel.   The plot was getting
thicker. John Rogers called Doc Taylor from the bedroom of Paul
Baresel's home. They chose that location because the princess
telephone on Baresel's bedside table was wide enough to
accommodate the suction cup which enabled the conversation to
be recorded. Taylor had to be located in a Dallas bank.

Rogers began the conversation by telling Taylor that he thought
the First National Bank would approve the loan but it was not
willing to act as trustee bank.

Taylor asked Rogers to approve an alternative trustee, the First
National Bank of Pekin, Illinois, where he had connections.
Taylor said he would fly to Pekin on January 2 to make the
necessary arrangements, and then come back on the 3rd.

Taylor asked, "Are you in your office?"

"No."

"Where are you?"

"I'm at my girl friend's house," Rogers replied. "Don't ask
me questions."

"Well, what I meant, can you talk?" Taylor asked.

"Yeah, sure, that's why I'm here."

"Okay. Well, then we don't have to guard anything."

Rogers asked, "Are you at a good phone?"

"Yeah. Yeah."

Rogers then brought up the matter of the payoff. "Alright.
Really, what I'm telling you is that I will write the letter based on
what I know the bank and the attorney general are going to do. So
what I was going to do is put it in your hot little hand and put a
check in your hand...."

"Okay."

"At the same time you bring the money, and you don't pay me,
you pay David."

"Yeah, I understand."

"But I'm not going to give you that letter until you bring what
you're supposed to bring."

"I understand," Taylor replied.

"Now, it's an eighth and a quarter," Rogers continued, "so I want to know how much it is."

Taylor suggested, "You tell me how much it is."

"Well, I think it's $31,250. Is that right?

"Well, you're the doctor. I thought that was for eight percent."

Rogers laughed. "You're going to get chintzy?" he asked.

"No, No," Taylor responded. "Absolutely not. Let me write it down so I won't forget it. Tell me again."

"$31,250."

"And that can be given to David?" Taylor inquired.

"But now, that's just half, Doc," Rogers added. "That's your first half, and when I get the $10 million paid to you, you have to come up with the other half."

"All right."

At no time in this or any other conversation did John Rogers suggest any payment to himself. Always, he insisted that the payment be made to David Hall, per FBI instructions. Moreover, Doc Taylor never questioned this arrangement.

                                    ...Tuesday, December 31, 1974

The Capitol.   The situation was getting more tense by the minute. Hall did *not* call John Rogers as promised--possibly because of Sanders' warning. Instead, he called Mooney and Taylor in Dallas and told them to go to a pay phone and call him back, which they did.

Taylor didn't much like the talk about Rogers "trying to set us up." That concerned him greatly.

Hall told them, "You know, there is a statute that says it's illegal to pay any money to John Rogers." They discussed the implications of that for a while.

It was hard for the investigators to figure out why they just didn't fold their tents and go home. Most people, if they were engaged in some nefarious activity, and somebody blew the whistle on it, would surely have bailed out in a New York minute. But they pressed on ahead.

Possibly for Taylor, anyway, the lure of money was just too

powerful. He stood to make a million dollars personally off this deal, Maybe that's why they stayed with it. As for Hall, maybe he fell victim to a syndrome that infects many public figures--they come to believe that they're invulnerable, that the law will never touch them. Mooney? One couldn't help feeling sorry for him; he was out of his league trying to run with these guys.

...Thursday, January 2, 1975
The Home of John Rogers.   Kevin Mooney called John Rogers at home to tell him that he and Taylor would not be up on the 3rd as planned because Hall was out of town. Rogers replied, "Well, I'm not going to do anything else until Hall comes and tells me what's going on."

Mooney called back again that evening and said he had talked to Taylor. He asked Rogers to "trust us," and he invited him to come to Dallas to see their operation. Rogers declined to do so.

...Friday, January 3, 1975
The Office of Secretary of State.   Kevin Mooney phoned John Rogers about mid-morning, very anxious. The offering circular for the project was now at the printer, but they could not complete the trust agreement portion of it without the preliminary commitment letter from Rogers. Mooney said he was flying to Oklahoma City that afternoon, and he wanted to pick up the letter and return it to Dallas.

As soon as he arrived at the Oklahoma City airport, Mooney called again. Rogers put him off. He refused to release the commitment letter to Mooney until he, Rogers, had a chance to discuss it with Hall.

Mooney then tried a different tack. He asked to take Rogers to dinner that evening. "I'll take you out to dinner and we'll talk about *your* deal," he suggested. That "deal" related to the discussion with Taylor back on December 18 regarding the manner of payment to Rogers, whereby Taylor might take care of the mortgage on a piece of Rogers' property.

Rogers declined, saying, "No dice. I don't want to have dinner with you."

...Saturday, January 4, 1975
The Home of John Rogers.   In an effort to turn up the heat, Rogers placed a telephone call to Doc Taylor in Dallas to ask where things stood. Taylor said the documents would be ready late on the 6th, but the bank in Pekin needed a preliminary commitment letter from Rogers before they could complete the trust agreement. Rogers played coy with his reply, causing Taylor to think perhaps he was holding out for an offer of more money.

Taylor ask Rogers to "trust us." He then proffered a suggestion that they form a business with Rogers and take care of him in that manner. "Help us, and we'll help you," he promised.

Listening to these taped conversations, it was clear to the investigators that John Rogers was playing a good con game. He had the fish securely on the hook. Now it was time to start reeling him in.

§ § §

6

The Sting

The Home of John Rogers. The biggest task now facing
Burkett and the FBI was to figure out a way to get the
co-conspirators to make the final, fatal step. They had no doubts
whatsoever as to Hall's guilt. But he remained an elusive target.
Despite all the recorded conversations of Rogers with Hall, Taylor
and Mooney, the investigators still did not have what they
considered to be a clear-cut and unambiguous statement from Hall
himself.

They had John Rogers call Hall at the governor's mansion and
try to get him on record as to the payoff matter. But Hall was
cagey--undoubtedly because of the warning from Sanders. He
refused to discuss the matter over the telephone; however, he did
suggest that Rogers should call him on Monday morning and set
up a time when they could get together in person.

...*Monday, January 6, 1975*
The Governor's Office. A strange meeting took place within
the confines of the governor's office. Hall would not talk aloud to
Rogers. Instead, he wrote a message on a 3x5 card for Rogers to
read. "We are bugged," it said.

Rogers wrote back, "How do you know?"

Hall wrote, "We have a monitoring system."

Hall wrote another message. "Wait eight months."

When Rogers left, he gave a note to Hall's secretary saying he didn't understand the situation, and he asked for a meeting in a safe place where they could talk.

Immediately, when Burkett learned about the note, he and Derryberry became concerned that there may be some truth to Hall's statement that there was a monitor in the governor's office. They called Roger Webb, Director of the Department of Public Safety, who arranged to meet them at the parking lot of the Lincoln Park Golf Course.

Webb used his car radio to get a highway patrol trooper who worked in the governor's office to come and meet them in the parking lot. The trooper assured them there was no such device, that Hall was lying.

That evening, Doc Taylor phoned Rogers at his home. He wanted to know about the meeting with the governor. Rogers told him that Hall wanted to wait eight months. Taylor replied that there had not been any discussion with Hall about delays.

Rogers ended the conversation by stating firmly that he was not going to do anything until he got his part. Taylor promised he would be back in touch.

...Tuesday, January 7, 1975
The State Capitol.　　　The investigative team was concerned that the project might get stalled. They needed to create a sense of urgency, so Rogers called Taylor in Dallas to say he'd just found out that the regular quarterly meeting of the trustees was set for the 8th of January. He said, "We need to act quickly."

Taylor called back in the afternoon. He said that the offering circular wasn't ready, but he expected the paperwork to be done and he would be in Oklahoma City by the 10th.

In the meantime, Burkett learned that James Cook, Commissioner of Charities and Corrections--who had strong reservations about the Taylor proposal--had now gone to the attorney general's office and asked for an opinion on how they could reverse the vote. This was a turn of events that Burkett and Derryberry hadn't counted on. At first, they were greatly concerned, but then they figured out a way to turn it into an advantage.

Rogers took a note to Governor Hall's office advising him of what Cook had done, and the fact that the board would meet the next morning. In it, he asked Hall to call two trustees and tell them to stay away from the meeting so as not to have enough members to constitute a quorum. Hall wasn't there, so Rogers left the note with Hall's secretary.

...Wednesday, January 8, 1975
The State Capitol. The meeting of the pension investment board was set for 9:30 a.m.. Only two trustees showed up. Lacking a quorum, the meeting was postponed.

Later that morning, John Rogers encountered David Hall in the Capitol parking lot. Instead of speaking, however, Hall motioned toward to his office.

Rogers got himself wired with the tape recorder, then went up to the governor's office. As before, Hall communicated by writing on 3x5 cards. He said Rogers was wrong about Cook.

"He's still with us," Hall wrote.

Rogers nodded.

Hall wrote, "Trust me."

"Wait eight months," he added.

The final message read, "Office bugged."

When they had finished, Hall took these notes, walked over to his toilet, set fire to them with a cigarette lighter and flushed them down the toilet. Interestingly, all these sounds were picked up by Rogers' body recorder.

...Friday, January 10, 1975
The Office of the Attorney General. Mooney walked unannounced into Rogers' office. He asked for, begged for, and pleaded for the commitment letter. Mooney asked Rogers to trust them and wait for his share until instructed by Hall. He suggested various alternative methods of payment. Rogers declined all of them. All this was recorded.

Mooney's assertions provided clear indication Hall was

involved from the beginning. They also confirmed that no payoff was made that day.

Rogers took Mooney to the attorney general's office where Mooney presented the completed trust agreement and offering circular. The attorney general later gave Rogers the form of an approval letter that needed only Rogers' signature.

That afternoon Hall talked briefly to Rogers in the hallway. Since this was Hall's last full working day in office, he was going through the Capitol building saying goodbye to people in the various offices. Hall whispered in Rogers' ear, "Trust them."

Rogers asked if they could be trusted--meaning Taylor and Mooney.

Hall whispered back, "I'm as sure of that as I am that the sun will come up tomorrow."

Mooney called Rogers at home that evening to report on his own conversations with Taylor and Hall. He indicated that Hall reported having spoken to Rogers as late as 3:00 that afternoon to assure him of his commitment but that a payment of $25,000 would be dangerous. The payoff deal was discussed, with Mooney reviewing what Hall and Taylor had said and acknowledging that Rogers wanted his money before he signed the commitment letter. Mooney furnished a Dallas telephone number for Hall and said he could be contacted there after 11:00 p.m.

Later that evening Rogers called Hall in Dallas. Hall engaged in a lot of doubletalk, but urged Rogers to sign the letter. He asked Rogers to trust him and wait for his share. He said he would talk again with Rogers on Monday morning.

...Sunday, January 12, 1975

The Home of John Rogers.   Late Sunday evening, Rogers received a telephone call at his home from Kevin Mooney. Mooney said he'd been called by "the fat man," meaning David Hall, who suggested that Mooney make this call.

Mooney sounded desperate. Once again, he asked Rogers to sign the letter, to trust them, and to wait for his payoff. Again, Rogers declined to wait for a delayed payoff, insisting he would only sign the letter when he got his money.

During the course of this conversation, Mooney made several incriminating statements that were recorded on tape, including the assertion that Hall "originated" the deal and that they were going to let Hall "complete the deal."

...Monday, January 13, 1975
The Office of the Governor.   The time had now come to spring the trap.

Rogers went into the governor's office to see Hall. It was not yet noon. As before, Hall would only communicate by written messages.

"Trust me," he wrote. "You must give the letter before you lose control."

Rogers wrote back, "I need some money now. After I sign the letter they won't take the chance, they don't need to, they won't do it in a safe way."

Hall wrote, "You can trust me, if they don't, I will pay your part personally. Depend on me only."

In a last-ditch effort to get Hall to incriminate himself on tape, Rogers called back to say he did not understand the messages. But Hall wouldn't talk on the telephone.

The next step was for Rogers to telephone Kevin Mooney and tell him the deal was on, which he did that evening. "We need to take this in our own hands and complete it," he said. Mooney agreed to locate Doc Taylor and have him call Rogers.

Taylor returned the call a few minutes later. He was at the Downtowner Motel in Jackson, Mississippi.

The message was the one Taylor had been waiting to hear: "Doc, I give up! Come get the letter."

Plans were made for Mooney to fly to Oklahoma City the next morning, arriving at 11:45 a.m. They agreed that Taylor would pay Mooney in the guise of "legal fees;" Mooney was to pay Hall, and Hall was to take care of Rogers. But Rogers said he needed $10,000 right away. Taylor promised, "I can get this in a few days. This is routine for us."

The Office of the Secretary of State.   Kevin Mooney found a big surprise in store for him when he came to Rogers' office. Several FBI agents were waiting in the anteroom. Of course, they didn't look like FBI agents; they were dressed to look like ordinary citizens who were there on routine business. Mooney didn't suspect a thing.

Rogers welcomed Mooney into his office and handed him the letter. He asked, "Where's the money? You were supposed to bring a check for $31,250." Rogers feigned disappointment when Mooney didn't have it. He then walked Mooney to the door.

When Kevin Mooney walked out of the door to the Secretary of State's office, he walked straight into the arms of the waiting FBI agents. He didn't say a word. He knew he'd been set up. They immediately placed him under arrest and whisked him downtown where he was booked, then released on bond.

At almost the same instant, another team of FBI agents was paying a visit to the Downtowner Motel in Jackson, Mississippi, where Doc Taylor was attending a meeting. They arrested him, booked him, and turned him loose on $25,000 bail. He flew back to Dallas that evening. His son-in-law, James Duckels, met him at the airport and drove him to his house.

The FBI did not search the contents of his wallet, otherwise they would have found the $31,250 check that he had written to Kevin Mooney. Taylor destroyed that damaging piece of evidence at his first opportunity after being released.

Nevertheless, Taylor still had a problem. Despite having destroyed one piece of incriminating evidence, there yet remained another, namely, the check stub in his check register. In an attempt to cover up this paper trail, he instructed Duckels to go down to his office and alter the stub to make it look like the $31,250 check had been written to someone else. Duckels did as he was told. He made a clumsy attempt to alter the stub to appear as if the check had been written to the Small Business Administration, and then, because of a mistake, had been voided out.

Taylor's lawyer, Emmett Colvin, found out what had been done. He blew his stack. "You can't do that!" he insisted. "You can't falsify records that way!"

So, poor Duckels traipsed back to the office and made a notation on the stub that it had originally been written to Kevin Mooney for "legal services." (This created another problem in that Kevin Mooney had never practiced law and was not licensed in the state of Texas.)

...Wednesday, January 15, 1975
The Office of the U.S. Attorney.   Kevin Mooney came to Bill Burkett's office with his lawyers, Rooney McInereny, a former supreme court justice, and Frank Keating, state senator and attorney from Tulsa. He was well represented. Mooney was ready to talk.

In their first conversation, Burkett told Mooney that he expected him to have a check for $31,250. Mooney said, "Taylor showed me that check."

Burkett sent the FBI to Taylor's office to look at the check register. That's when they found the altered stub. That was a very damaging piece of evidence. Taylor hadn't volunteered the information, of course, nor was he required to. But his attorney, Emmett Colvin, took the position that if the government found it, they found it; but at least he wasn't going to let his client destroy evidence.

...Thursday, January 16, 1975
The Federal Courthouse.   David Hall was indicted on four counts of bribery and extortion. He was charged with extorting $50,000 from W. W. Taylor and R. Kevin Mooney, conspiracy to attempt to bribe Secretary of State John Rogers, and two separate violations involving interstate facilities.

Taylor was indicted on charges of conspiracy to attempt bribery and also two separate violations involving interstate facilities.

Mooney was initially charged on three counts, but Burkett agreed to drop two counts in exchange for his guilty plea in the conspiracy charge and his testimony.

At the time of his arraignment, Hall told reporters, "I wish the trial were tomorrow so I could prove my innocence."

A few days earlier, Bill Burkett, O. B. Johnston III, Jim Peters, Jack DeWitt, Paul Baresel, and John Rogers held a discussion in Burkett's office about what would be the best day to issue the indictments. They didn't want to indict Hall on Inauguration Day, January 13th, because it would steal headlines from the new governor, David Boren. In his mind's eye, Burkett could just see pictures on the front page of the *Daily Oklahoman* of David Boren taking the oath of office with an empty chair on the podium, captioned, "That's where the ex-governor would have sat, but he was in jail."

They decided on the 14th, the day after leaving office. However, the Department of Justice called from Washington, D.C., saying the United States Attorney General had a major press conference scheduled; would they mind delaying the indictment one more day? They agreed. After all, there wasn't really any reason to hurry the indictment.

That afternoon O.B. Johnston III came into Burkett's office and announced, "Your phone is bugged."

"Why?" Burkett asked.

"I just talked to Jack Taylor, investigative reporter for the *Daily Oklahoman*, and he knew that we were delaying the indictment."

Immediately Burkett got on the phone to the Justice Department. "How do I find out if my telephone is bugged?" Before they could respond, a thought struck him. "Wait a minute," Burkett said. "Let me call you back."

He hung up the phone and got ahold of John Rogers. "John," he asked, "have you talked to Jack Taylor today?"

"No...well...I had lunch with him." Aha! That was the source! Rogers talked to everybody! His tongue was loose at both ends, and he was incapable of keeping a secret.

Somewhat chagrined, Burkett called the Department back and

told them to forget about checking his phone, that he figured out where the leak came from.

The team also had quite a debate over what to do about the bribery charges still pending from the year-long grand jury investigations. Burkett took the position that they had such a strong case here that it was more important to concentrate on this trial than it was to pursue the earlier grand jury investigation.

That didn't mean they planned to drop the earlier charges, however; it just meant that they were going to put the charges on "hold" for the time being. The U.S. Attorney would still be free to bring them up again at a time of his own choosing.

It was ironic, therefore, the misdeeds that brought David Hall to the U.S. Attorney's attention were not the charges on which he would be tried. Burkett went for the sure conviction.

§ § §

7

Pre-Trial Maneuvering

...Friday, January 17, 1975
The Office of the U.S. Attorney.   Burkett' team of prosecutors began the arduous task of getting ready for trial. The tapes, of course, were seen to be the key.

The matter was complicated somewhat by David Hall who, at his arraignment, asked for a speedy trial. A date was set for February 24, scarcely a month away. That didn't allow much time for transcribing the mountain of tapes.

Burkett knew there would be a knock-down, drag-out battle over those tapes. The defense team would use every tactic they could to keep them from being introduced into evidence. So, as soon as duplicate copies could be run off, a complete set of recordings was given to the defense. Then the prosecution set about the task of preparing written transcripts from the tapes.

It was a big job. The secretaries in the U.S. Attorney's office and the FBI office worked nearly full time on the transcripts. They even borrowed the secretary of Appellate Judge Bill Holloway.

Some of the tapes were good and clear, and some were not. These women were listening to them and doing the best they could, typing what they thought they heard, and receiving little assistance from the agents or attorneys. Consequently, not being familiar with the voices of the various individuals involved, they made many mistakes--frequently attributing something said to the wrong person. Moreover, some of the recordings contained gaps and unintelligible passages.

Initially, the defense had agreed to work with Burkett in perfecting the transcripts. It seemed that it would be in everybody's best interest to have a reasonably accurate transcription. But once they heard what was on the tapes, that agreement went out the window; they wanted no part of assisting anybody in knowing what was said.

...January-February, 1975

The Players.   D. C. Thomas, attorney for David Hall, was a prominent criminal lawyer. That's all that he did--practice criminal law. He didn't do civil work. Like any good trial lawyer, he had developed ploys and stratagems over the years that he used over and over again. Thomas was a little taller than average, in his late forties, with a solid build and dark hair combed straight back.

Burkett had been in court a few times with D. C. over the years. He had come to respect his quick mind and scrupulous honesty. D. C. was personally one of the funniest people in the defense bar. His style was folksy, disarming, and exhibited a flair for the dramatic, but he used a lot of sarcasm in the courtroom, particularly when questioning a hostile witness. Whatever his style, one could count on Thomas to be totally prepared and as tenacious as a bulldog.

Jack Dawson, the second member of Hall's defense team, was a young lawyer from Thomas's office, not long out of law school, and was there primarily for the learning experience. He was fairly tall, nice-looking, and did not dress to extreme. In Burkett's view, many of the issues argued at the bench went over Dawson's head; but, again, he was new to the work of lawyering and this was a pretty big case.

Most prominent among the lawyers was James Paul ("Jimmy") Linn, representing W. W. Taylor. Linn, 49, a brilliant trial lawyer, was tall, handsome, and very smooth. He was good friends with Burkett, but they had never been in court with or against each other. However, friendship would not play a role inside the courtroom. Jimmy Linn had his job to do and Burkett had his job to do, and no quarter would be given by either party.[1]

John Michael ("Mike") Johnson was another young lawyer fresh out of law school. Johnson was a short fellow, blond haired, and a natty dresser. He was used mainly as a "gofer" and did not contribute greatly to the case.

Emmett Colvin was the third member of Taylor's defense team. In his late fifties, Colvin was tall, balding, courtly, scholarly, very respectful and low key. He was a prominent criminal defense lawyer from Dallas, Texas, and he argued most of the motions before the judge.

The hallmark of Colvin, Burkett's mind, lay in the fact of what he told Taylor about the altered check stub. He had a great respect for the law.

Bill Burkett led the prosecution, of course. With six years under his belt as U.S. Attorney, coupled with his previous experience as county attorney, he was superbly versed in the art of prosecution. He received his LL.B. and J.D. from the University of Oklahoma Law School.

The other two members of the prosecution team were Jim Peters and O. B. Johnston III. Peters, 41, was of medium height, round-faced, thinning hair, good sense of humor--and a new father. He had come to the office from the state highway department where he handled land condemnation cases. Although he had no previous criminal background, Peters was very meticulous, conscientious and smart, and he fit right in. What a lawyer needs to succeed is some incisiveness, and Peters had it; he could take a set of facts, quickly identify what the issue was, and determine what needed to be done.

Johnston was 33, a graduate from Baylor University and Tulsa University Law School. He had just come out of the army Judge Advocate General (JAG) in 1970 when Burkett hired him to replace John Sparks who left go into practice with his father in Woodward. O. B.'s wife was the daughter of Paul Darrough, long-time U.S. Bankruptcy judge. Johnston handled both civil and criminal cases and was a very aggressive trial lawyer.

In addition, Burkett utilized two young attorneys, Drew Neville and Bill Price. Both lawyers had only been with the office for less than a month. They were there primarily for the training; neither participated much in the trial. Neville had been a legislative assistant to Senator Henry Bellmon in Washington; Price was the son of Dr. Joel Price, a wealthy physician who owned widespread oil and gas interests throughout the state.

The man whose luck it fell to be the presiding judge was the Honorable Fred Daugherty. Frederick Alvin Daugherty, age 60, was born in Oklahoma City, graduated from Oklahoma City University, and received his law degree from Cumberland University. A highly decorated officer in the Pacific Theater during World War II, he later commanded the 179th Infantry Regiment in combat in the Korean War, and later rose to command of the famed 45th Infantry Division with the rank of major general. Tall, trim, iron-gray hair, with finely-chiseled features, he radiated an air of quiet self-confidence. Daugherty was a superb jurist and the ideal judge for this kind of case--totally unflappable, twenty years on the bench, experienced in high-profile cases, and at the height of his powers. He entered the practice of law in 1947, and after a two-year hiatus during the Korean War, he received his first judicial appointment in 1955 as a district judge in state court; in 1961 he moved to the federal bench, and for the last three years served as the chief judge of the Western District.

...Sunday, January 19, 1975

Sunday Oklahoman.   David Hall was not without his political allies. For example, Tom Steed, Democratic U.S. Representative from the 4th District, launched a public attack on Burkett personally. ''They've been dragging him [Hall] around for months and months,'' he complained in a telephone interview from his Washington, D.C., office. He threatened that if there was no guilty verdict, he would call for a congressional investigation.

The congressman accused Burkett of using the grand jury and his office to play partisan politics. ''You just don't go on for months leaking stuff to the press and smearing stuff around without a case."

In response, Burkett challenged Steed to pay a visit to his office, but not for a social call. The purpose of that visit would be for Steed to look at the evidence that the prosecution had put together and to turn up any evidence that the U.S. Attorney's office had been playing politics or abusing power.

"If it develops that we have played politics or abused the power of the office,... then I'll take appropriate action and make it public," Burkett offered. "On the other hand, if Mr. Steed doesn't find any evidence, then I'll expect him to apologize."

Steed never took up the offer.

...Tuesday, January 21, 1975
The Federal Courthouse.   Kevin Mooney entered a plea of guilty to the conspiracy count. It was a plea bargain. The other two counts were dismissed.

Burkett recommended to Judge Daugherty that Mooney receive probation, but the judge said, "I don't even think about the sentencing until I've seen the pre-sentence report." All Burkett could do was recommend; the matter was entirely in the judge's hands.

The Federal Rules of Criminal Procedure requires the judge to enter into a colloquy directly with the defendant. The purpose is to establish the factual basis of the plea and also to make sure the defendant understands exactly what the charge is and the effects of his plea.

Co-defendants David Hall and W. W. Taylor stood beside Mooney as he entered his plea. According to courtroom observers, Hall reacted visibly.

THE COURT: "The Court asks you whether you received any promises of any kind from anybody to cause you to plead guilty to count two of the indictment?"

MOONEY: "I received none, Your Honor."

THE COURT: "Beginning on or about September 1, 1974, and continuing thereafter to on or about January 16, 1975, the date of the return of this indictment, did you and your co-defendants in said count two knowingly, willfully, unlawfully, and feloniously conspire with each other to commit an offense against the United States, this being to travel in interstate commerce and... did you do this with intent to promote, manage, establish, carry on, and facilitate...an unlawful activity?''

MOODY: "Yes, sir.''

THE COURT: "Was this unlawful activity a scheme to bribe a public officer or public officers of the State of Oklahoma for the purpose of influencing the Board of Trustees of the system to invest ten million dollars of the funds of the system with Guaranteed Investors Corporation?''

MOODY: "Yes, Your Honor.''

THE COURT: "Was it part of this conspiracy that the three defendants agreed among themselves that Taylor and Mooney would pay to Hall the sum or $50,000?''

MOONEY: "Yes, Your Honor.''

THE COURT: "Was it a further part of this conspiracy that the defendant Hall would, by reason of his official position, influence other members of said Board to act favorably upon the investment proposal made by you and defendant Taylor to the Board?''

MOONEY: "Yes, Your Honor.''

Naturally, the news media covered the proceeding and avidly reported it in great detail. The publicity that followed, as one might expect, was mostly unfavorable to Hall and Taylor. After all, here was a co-conspirator spelling out the terms of a criminal conspiracy that involved a former governor of the state during his term in office.

...Friday, February 7, 1975
The Courtroom.   Judge Daugherty held a hearing on two major motions filed by the defense. The first was to move the trial to another district on the grounds of prejudicial publicity that would prevent Hall from getting a fair trial in this district. Coupled with this was a motion for continuance. Hall's attorneys alleged that information had been selectively leaked to friendly

reporters by the U.S. Attorney's office in order to try Hall in the newspapers.

Their second motion was to suppress the tapes on the grounds that they had been obtained illegally. Nothing unusual there. It's a common defense tactic to attack evidence on the grounds it was illegally obtained.

Daugherty wasn't buying. With regard to prejudicial publicity--the first motion--Judge Daugherty proclaimed at the outset that he thought the real test was the impact of the publicity on prospective jurors. He said, "I'm also not convinced that I need any people to tell me that in their opinion this publicity, such as you lay before me, will not afford anybody a fair trial. Because here again, the acid test is when you put jurors in the box, to see if they can give a fair trial under proper *voir dire*."[2]

D. C. Thomas, however, continued to belabor the point. "Your Honor, it's difficult if... they have been exposed to incidents, to experiences, to thoughts and philosophies in life... to be fair and impartial. And that's what concerns me about this pre-trial publicity."

Judge Daugherty was not swayed. He pointed out that the logic of Thomas's argument would mean "...a prominent person could never go to trial.... You could never have tried some of the famous crimes in history, such as the assassination of Senator Kennedy and others."

"Yes, sir," Thomas said. Thomas said he had witnesses present to speak on this matter. The judge said he would listen to a limited number of them.

Jimmy Linn did not view pre-trial publicity as big an issue as Thomas did--or perhaps he felt the judge's opinion was a foregone conclusion--but he did seize this occasion to ask the court to permit the lawyers to participate in the *voir dire* questioning of the jury. Linn was asking Judge Daugherty to bend the rules. In federal court, unlike state courts, only the judge asks questions of prospective jurors. Each side can submit questions to the judge that they want posed to the jurors, but the judge does the questioning. (Most lawyers like to ask questions of the jurors because it lets them educate the jurors about their case.)

Judge Daugherty said he was not prepared to make a ruling yet. He said he thought the motion was premature but that he would listen to a couple of witnesses and look at the publicity.

"May we have your evidence now?" the judge asked, seeking to move things along.

"Yes, your Honor," Thomas replied. "For my first witness, I call Mr. Watson."

James V. Watson of Yukon, Oklahoma, took the stand. He was the publisher of the *Mustang Mirror* and the *Yukon Review*. Watson was handed a packet of newspaper articles from the *Daily Oklahoman*, the *Oklahoma City Times*, and the *Oklahoma Journal*. Under questioning from Thomas, he said he'd read most of those articles and had tried to keep his finger on the pulse of his community by talking and corresponding with his readers. Thomas asked him what the general opinion was regarding David Hall.

"I think most people feel that he's guilty," Watson replied.

Thomas then asked, "Do you have an opinion as to whether or not David Hall could receive a fair and impartial trial in the Western District of Oklahoma at this time?"

"I don't think he could."

On cross examination, Watson acknowledged that David Hall had called him and asked him to come and testify, and that he personally thought Hall was innocent. Burkett asked him how he had collected his information about people's opinions.

A: "Just from visits in the coffee shop and conversations with people who drop by my office."

Q: "Could you tell me who they are, sir?"

A: "Well, normally, there's two of us, that's Mr. Love, from the Yukon Furniture Mart, and generally a number of others..."

Q: "Who has dropped by your office and you visited with about this since this indictment was returned?"

A: "Well, Elvus Sasseen, Don Copeland--"

Q: "Elvus Sasseen? What's his business?"

A: "I think he's an insurance agent."

Watson said he *thought* that Sasseen thought Hall was guilty, but he didn't know what Copeland's opinion was. He could not remember anyone else he had talked to about this deal.

Thomas then called as his second witness James C. Nance, 81, an old-time politician and publisher of the *Purcell Register*. Nance was a pitiable character on the stand; he testified that he was a constant reader of the *Oklahoman* and *Times*, and that he had read the *Journal* since it began publication. He said that public sentiment had been turned against David Hall by the continuous pounding of certain newspapers on the governor and his official life by slanted news stories.

On cross examination, Burkett asked Nance which newspaper had accused him of receiving kickbacks.

"Well, the *Daily Oklahoman*, it's the king bee, one of the first. He's been accused of taking kickbacks, he's been accused of controlling contracts...."

When asked if he'd read the news stories that were in the packet, Nance launched into a long, rambling tirade. "Well, I've read a great many of them all the while, all through. The *Daily Oklahoman* took off on Hall, if you remember, to build prejudice against him before he was ever inducted into office. They pursued him in the campaign, they pursued him in the contest. They opened up against him before he was ever inaugurated and they pursued him all during these years with everything they could that converted, slanted or degrade him, weaken him."

"Could you show us one of the slanted stories?" Burkett asked.

"Well, all of them. All of them."

When Nance finished, Judge Daugherty decided he had heard enough. He declined to hear the testimony of any of the other reporters that Thomas had lined up.

The court heard the lawyers' arguments. Thomas felt the articles were prejudicial on their face. Linn argued that there had been prejudicial publicity, but he didn't point out any specific examples. He said that *voir dire* would be the true test, and he urged the court to give prospective jurors a complete *voir dire* examination.

Burkett argued that "at most the evidence shows that Hall can't get a fair trial in the coffee shop in Yukon or the bank in Purcell," and that neither of these is a "court town."[3] The rule says that the court must satisfy itself that the defendant cannot get a fair and impartial trial in any of the court towns before it can transfer the trial outside the district. Neither defendant had made any showing that Hall couldn't get a fair trial in any of those twelve cities.

Judge Daugherty recessed to read the press clippings.

The hearing resumed at 1:30. Judge Daugherty ruled against the motion to dismiss the indictment based on alleged prejudicial pre-trial publicity. He decreed, "The court is aware of no authority that says that an indictment must be dismissed and the defendant thereby not prosecuted on the basis of what might be termed pre-trial publicity."

As to the motions for a continuance or a transfer, he denied these motions also but said he would reconsider them again "at the forthcoming effort to impanel a fair and impartial jury."

Judge Daugherty then took up the defense motions to suppress the tapes.

D. C. Thomas introduced David Austern of Washington, D.C., to join the counsel for the defense. This was the first time the prosecution had heard of him.

Austern was in his mid-thirties, nice-looking, stocky, aggressive, and obviously knew what he was doing. He was a former Justice Department attorney brought in solely to help in the attack on the tapes. He seemed very knowledgeable about government agency investigative procedures--things that ordinary attorneys wouldn't be likely to know.

The first witness was John Rogers. To the layman, it may seem strange that the prosecution's main witness for the trial should be called by the other side as their witness, but that's the way the judicial process works sometimes. The defense set out to convince the judge of two things, (1) that John Rogers was coerced into cooperating--i.e., that he did not voluntarily participate, and (2) that the evidence was obtained by illegal means. Along the way, they hoped to "discover" any additional evidence the government might have on their clients.[4]

D. C. Thomas conducted the direct examination of Rogers. He tediously and endlessly walked Rogers through an identification of all of the telephones by number and address on which the devices had been placed to record the conversations. But when Thomas tried to get into the nature of the conversations, Burkett rose to object. Judge Daugherty sustained the objection and limited Thomas only to the issue of legality or illegality, saying, "I will not... let you get into the details of the evidence as to who may or may not have talked, what was said, who was called, so forth."

When Thomas persisted with the same line of questioning, the judge made it clear that this hearing was not concerned with what was said in the conversations, only whether the tapes were illegally obtained. "Show me an illegal wiretap and I will throw the evidence out," he said. "But you've got to show me an illegal wiretap and that's the purpose of this hearing, not to get at the content of them."

Thomas argued that he was only trying to discover if there were any tapes of other persons that he didn't have.

Daugherty framed the issue more sharply, "You have the burden to show that the alleged wiretapping was illegal. After all, you have legal wiretapping as well as illegal wiretapping. You have the burden to show it's illegal. If it's illegal, then I will suppress it."[5]

Not making any headway with this line of questioning, Thomas turned next to the matter of a 1972 IRS investigation of Rogers which was concluded in February of 1974, and an SEC investigation of a company in which Rogers was involved in 1967. Again, Thomas sought to imply that these cases were probably still hanging over Rogers' head and, therefore, his consent to cooperating with the U.S. Attorney's office was coerced by threats of reopening these issues. Thomas had no evidence of this; he didn't even make the allegation that such was the case; rather, he just went into it hoping to dig up something that would help his case.

Jimmy Linn took over the questioning. He was not able to get even a hint of any kind of coercion, but nonetheless he worked over those IRS and SEC investigations *ad nauseam*. He tried to make a big deal out of a "non-prosecution" letter Burkett had written Rogers in December, but that, too, fell flat. He asked Rogers to recount his conversation with FBI agent Ted Rosack regarding his consent to be taped. Rogers said he told Rosack, "Sure, if it's legal." He said he assumed the FBI wouldn't be doing it if it wasn't legal.

Burkett cross examined Rogers on his consent and had him state specifically that none of the investigations, nor the non-prosecution letter, nor any civil audit, nor any coercions or threats in any way impacted on his consent, that it was free and voluntary. That exchange pretty much laid that issue to rest.

At this point, and before bringing any more witnesses, Burkett argued to the court that there was no "substance to this complaint on the part of the defendants," that "not a one of them ever asked [John Rogers] if he consented voluntarily," and that he was still waiting to "hear an allegation from the defendants that there is something illegal."

Daugherty said to the defense, "I told you where the burden rests and I'm frank to say that thus far I have received no evidence of an illegal wiretap. Now, if I'm going to suppress evidence of an illegal wiretap, I've got to have proof that it was an illegal wiretap." Nevertheless, and despite the defense's failure to make any such allegation, Daugherty went on to say he was willing to hear from investigative agencies so that the court could "rest assured that there is no such illegally obtained evidence."

This exchange instilled in Burkett a greater appreciation of Judge Daugherty. The judge gave the defense a full hearing. Time and again Burkett said, "Judge they haven't alleged... they haven't even made the claim." Ordinarily, when one is offering evidence, he is limited to evidence that supports what he has alleged to be the facts. But Judge Daugherty would reply, "Yes I know that. You're probably right, Mr. Burkett, but I want to make sure that we get to the bottom of this and get it all out in the open."

Judge Daugherty was always conscious of the trial record and of the appellate judges who almost certainly would one day be asked to read it.[6] Daugherty's high reputation among jurists was based in part on his careful attention to such matters. Burkett, of course, was eternally glad that he did this because when it came time for appeal, the defense had nothing they could legally complain about. Judge Daugherty leaned over backwards to hear everything they wanted to put on.

After a short recess, Burkett called Larry Naiser, the Chief Intelligence Agent of the IRS for the Oklahoma City District. The hour was now 4:00 p.m. John Rogers had been on the stand over two hours.

Direct examination of Naiser took less than a minute.

Q: "Has the Internal Revenue Service conducted any kind of electronic surveillance pertaining to the violations which are set forth in the indictment in the case now in hearing?"

A: "We have nothing to do with it, sir."

Q: "Have you furnished any information to the Department of Justice, or any of its representatives, that pertain to this case?"

A: "No, sir."

Q: "Then, it would follow that there have been no electronic surveillances conducted by the Internal Revenue Service that pertained to this case, is that correct?"

A: "That's correct."

David Austern, who was brought in by the defense for just this purpose, conducted the cross examination. It soon became apparent that he was not there merely to wage war on the tapes, he was also trying to compel some "discovery"--finding out what other evidence the government might have on Hall or Taylor.

Austern asked, "Mr. Naiser, at any time, to your knowledge,

has the intelligence division of the Internal Revenue Service conducted electronic surveillance on David Hall?''

Burkett objected that the question was irrelevant and immaterial. The judge overruled, explaining that if the government *did* do any illegal wiretapping, they may have gotten information that led to something in this case; and if that [IRS electronic surveillance] was illegally obtained information, then it could affect the legality of evidence in this case. That principle is called the ''fruit of the poisonous tree;'' to wit, one cannot use any leads or anything else that he acquired from illegally obtained evidence.

When Austern re-asked that question, Naiser said, ''I have obtained authorization to testify as to this particular case that's before us and no other authorization at this time.''

At this point, Judge Daugherty called the attorneys to the bench. He wanted Burkett to call and get permission for Naiser to answer this question.

''Your Honor,'' Burkett objected, ''this is just a pure fishing expedition by Mr. Thomas and his co-counsel here; it has nothing to do with this case whatsoever.''

''Mr. Burkett,'' the judge said, ''I understand you're probably on solid ground and I could halt the whole thing now but as I've already indicated to you, I just like a good clean record here that we have no wiretap in this case.''

Naiser was excused to call Washington to seek permission to disclose any information about other electronic surveillance on Hall.

Burkett asked the court for permission to put on another witness while waiting for Naiser to make his calls. Paul Baresel took the witness stand. Baresel testified that he had first talked to John Rogers on the 9th of December; that Rogers consented to the taping; that he, Baresel, supervised it and that agents DeWitt and Dwight Garretson assisted him; that the telephone conversations were on a Sony tape recorder attached to the phone by either a suction cup or an induction coil on the receiver; that personal conversations were recorded by a tape recorder concealed in John's clothing and at times he had a transmitter on his body that broadcast to FBI agents within a one- or two-block radius; that John was a party to all of the conversations taped except one between Marvin Emerson, Assistant Attorney General, and Kevin Mooney; and that a copy of all tapes had been furnished to the defense except for one that was very weak and had to be sent to Washington for the lab to try to enhance the sound level.

Again, the cross examination was conducted by David Austern. Under Austern's questioning, Baresel testified that no other recordings of the defendants were made in this case. Once again, Austern tried to find out what other evidence may have been gathered.

Q: "Had you searched or has anyone under your authority or working with you, searched the records of the FBI to determine whether at any time electronic surveillance was made of David Hall or any other defendant in this case?"

A: "No, sir."

Q: "Do you know, from your own knowledge, whether a search has been made of the files and records of any other federal enforcement agency?"

A: "No, sir."

Q: "Do you know whether a search has been made of any state enforcement agency in the State of Oklahoma to determine whether or not electronic surveillance has been made?"

A: "No, sir."

Baresel's questioning ended with his testifying that John Rogers had signed consent forms for each and every taping, and that no tapes were missing, misplaced or lost. At that point, Burkett put copies of all of the consent forms into evidence.

By then, Larry Naiser had come back to the courtroom and was ready to resume his testimony. Austern continued his cross examination.

Q: "Has the defendant David Hall been the subject of any electronic surveillance at any time by the intelligence division of the IRS?"

A: "Yes, sir. In November of 1973 we taped three telephone conversations between David Hall and Dorothy Pike, with consent of Dorothy Pike."

He said they had no tapes of W. W. Taylor.

Burkett offered transcripts of those three telephone conversations into evidence for the judge to examine *in camera,* meaning, in his chambers. If the judge found anything questionable, then he would show them to the defense; otherwise, not.

Burkett also gave the court Paul Baresel's "302"--his report of the meeting of the 9th of December. Austern asked the court to require the government to make a search of responsible state authorities to see if any tapes had been made of the defendants.

Naiser was excused. There were no more witnesses.

The hour was late, but Austern continued to urge that the "government be directed to make a search of all federal and state authorities to find out if any information had been taken by way of electronic surveillance, or leads therefrom."

"What about city, county, highway patrol and ad infinitum?" the judge asked sardonically.

Austern jokingly alluded to a situation involving the CIA some months before in which somebody should have made a search of the records.

Daugherty was not amused. "I'm not going to require every last possible agency who does law enforcement work to be exhausted from shore to shore before I'm going to be satisfied. I remind you, Counsel, I stated it earlier, that the initial burden is on you. *The defendant in a criminal case who asserts that evidence against him was improperly obtained by wiretapping has the burden of proving to the trial court's satisfaction the truth of the assertion.* That is the United States Supreme Court speaking. I would suggest that I don't think you have in any sense met this burden at this point."

The judge's point was clear and unmistakable: the prosecution didn't have to do anything to prove the tapes were legal; if the defense makes an attack on the evidence, then the burden is on them to prove that the tapes are illegal. Following that pronouncement, he recessed the court to give himself an opportunity to read the transcripts of those tapes. The judge said he would have a ruling by Monday.

...Monday, February 10, 1975

The Courtroom.   The defendants filed a motion to dismiss the indictment on the grounds that it was duplicitous. Daugherty denied the defense motions to continue, transfer and suppress.

...Tuesday, February 11, 1975

The Courtroom.   Daugherty denied the motion to dismiss. He did order the prosecution, on the 12th, to give the defendants transcripts of the grand jury testimony leading to the indictment. This involved the testimony of John Rogers, Jim Cook, and L. P. Williams.

Ordinarily, grand jury testimony is secret and not available to the defense unless they make a showing of what's called particularized need.

The defense hadn't make any such showing. But apparently Daugherty simply wanted to give them everything so they wouldn't have any basis for appeal.

§ § §

8

The Prosecution - Act I

...Monday, February 24, 1975
The Courtroom.   The courtroom is laid out like a cathedral.
Members of the public are the congregation, and they are always
divided from the clergy by a railing, called the "bar." The jury
box takes the place of the choir stalls. In this trial, the jury box is
on the left. The raised altar at the back is the province of the
judge, the high priest of the Law. The witness chair is between
the judge and the jury.
   This courtroom is larger than the others. It is the Ceremonial
Courtroom which is used for ceremonial occasions, swearing in of
new judges and U.S. Attorneys, and for particularly well-attended
trials such as this one. The bench is larger than normal, capable of
seating nine or ten judges at ceremonial events. It is the
courtroom of the chief judge--who, at this time, was Fred
Daugherty.
   The middle area is dominated by two large polished oak tables,
one on each side. Seated at the table on the left--the one nearest
the jury box--were the lawyers for the prosecution: Bill Burkett,
Jim Peters, and O. B. Johnston III. The table on the right was
occupied by the two defendants, David Hall and W. W. Taylor,
together with their attorneys D. C. Thomas and Jack Dawson
representing Hall; and Jimmy Linn, Mike Johnston and Emmett
Colvin representing Taylor. Behind each table stacks of boxes
contained documents that the lawyers would use during the trial.

In the center was the podium from which the lawyers would speak and conduct their questioning of witnesses.

No matter how many times one has been in court, the start of a new trial is always an exciting and frightening experience.

The first order of business was the selection of a jury. Surprisingly, jury selection went quickly and easily. By the time the court recessed for lunch twelve citizens "good and true" were impaneled, along with two alternate jurors.

The jury was comprised of seven men and five women: Ricky D. Creed, Lillie M. Knox, Richard E. Kinnard, James W. Bruner, Priscilla M. Doss, Albert F. LaMonte, Ruth H. Jones, Dorothy L. Vincent, Preston R. Kelly, Jerry M. Bastion, Dell Meyer, and Claud A. Cundiff. The two alternates were Berry H. Gentry and Fred B. Tapp.

As soon as the jury was seated, D. C. Thomas made a motion that the jury be sequestered--kept apart from public view--for the duration of the trial. He argued that they would be "exposed to extreme, heavily prejudicial news coverage, TV coverage and radio coverage."

Burkett objected saying, "Your Honor, I would only say that the jury is going to hear from the witness stand far more items that bear as to prejudice... than they are to receive from the news media."

Motion denied.

"Now, Ladies and Gentlemen of the jury," began Judge Daugherty, "you're the jury that will be trying this case. "First, the Court instructs you that you will not discuss the case amongst yourselves as jurors at any time while you're sitting on the case, prior to the time the case is submitted to you and you are escorted to the Jury Deliberation Room to consider your verdicts.

"Next, the Court instructs you that you are not to discuss the case with anyone not a member of the jury at any time while you're sitting on the case as juror...

"It is your duty, as jurors, to decide this case strictly on the evidence and the law as given to you here in the courtroom.

"Lastly, the Court instructs you, now, to keep your minds free and open and do not form any opinions about the case until you have heard all the evidence, until you have heard all the arguments of counsel and the instructions of the Court as to the law of this case."

When the principals returned from lunch, and the jurors had taken their places, it was time for the opening arguments to begin.

The opening statement is a lawyer's opportunity to tell the jury what his evidence will show. It is extremely important because the evidence doesn't always come in chronological order. But by providing the jury with this "big picture," as he sees it, the lawyer prepares the jury to fit together the various bits and pieces of evidence that may be presented out of chronological order, and to understand the importance of each piece of evidence. The lawyer may not argue the case in his opening statement; he may only tell the jury what the evidence will show.

One school of thought says you win or lose a case on your opening statement. Although Burkett didn't believe that opinion to be true, he nevertheless agreed that the opening statement is very important and he gave it a lot of attention.

The prosecution always goes first. In his opening statement, Burkett began by telling the jury he was giving them the "big picture," and, having heard the prosecution's statement of the whole case, they would be able to fit into place the evidence as it comes to them from the witness stand and the exhibits that are admitted.

Next, he identified by name and role all of the individuals that they would see and hear during this trial. Then he walked through chronologically the entire sequence of events leading up to the arrests of David Hall and W. W. Taylor.

Finally, he summarized by saying, "The evidence will show, Ladies and Gentlemen, that John Rogers' actions, taken after he came to the FBI, were part of a plan laid out for him; that most of these conversations, after the 12th of December were recorded. Some of them are of poor quality. When we have shown you this evidence, we will ask that you find both defendants guilty as charged.''

Jimmy Linn's opening statement was fairly short. He told the jury that Doc Taylor was a businessman with a good reputation, and he had a good plan which would have made the fund more money than it had ever made before.

"The first time he ever met John Rogers," Linn said, "John Rogers asked for money," and that Rogers was "demanding incessantly, continually, 'Give me money, money, money.'" The worst thing that Doc Taylor ever did wrong, according to Linn, was to lead John Rogers on.

Linn told the jurors that Rogers couldn't approve or disapprove this plan but he could kill it by making sure that it wasn't presented to the people who had the power to pass it.

Linn sought to discredit Rogers by saying Rogers had an interest in seeing Hall convicted because he himself was in serious trouble with the government, having invoked the Fifth Amendment with the grand jury. He said that Rogers thought that the tax people were on him, that he had high political ambitions, and he saw this as a way to rehabilitate himself. He said Rogers had been granted immunity by the government, and therefore they just shouldn't believe John Rogers.

D. C. Thomas, Hall's attorney, reserved his opening statement, which was his prerogative. He preferred to save his opening statement until that point in the trial when he began the defense of his client.

The time was a little past 4:00. Rather than get into the first witness this late in the day, the court recessed until 9:30 Tuesday morning.

...Tuesday, February 25, 1975
The Courtroom.   A chill February wind had blown in from the Rockies, and the lawyers tamped their feet as they removed their hats, coats and gloves.

The government called its first witness, Kevin Mooney. To

begin, Burkett wanted the jury to hear how long Mooney had known David Hall. Mooney said they had gone to law school together, and he had maintained a social acquaintance with Hall over the years.

Then he wanted the jury to know, "Have you ever practiced law, Mr. Mooney?"

"I have not."

That question set an important point that Burkett would use later on when it came time to discuss the $31,250 check written to him by Taylor, ostensibly for legal services.

Mooney testified that he called Hall, a social call, about the middle of October, 1974, to ask what he intended to do upon leaving office. About a week later, Hall phoned back to say he wanted to meet with Mooney--that he was en route to Houston and was stopping off at Meacham Field in Fort Worth in the highway patrol plane. Hall told Mooney that he intended to practice law and deal in real estate; and he showed Mooney plans for a resort development project in California called Palo Mesa for which he was seeking financing.

About a week after that, Mooney testified, Hall again called him to ask if he found anybody who could handle the project. Mooney said he told Hall about W. W. Taylor, a man with whom he worked and who was in the business of finding money. He recommended Taylor highly. Hall said he would like to meet the man. Hall suggested they come to Oklahoma City, have dinner, and discuss the project.

At this point, Burkett wanted the jury to hear about Hall's use of a state airplane for private purposes--not that it had anything to do with guilt or innocence in this case, but to reveal the man's character. He asked Mooney, "How did you get to Oklahoma City?"

A: "We were picked up at Love Field, Dallas, by a highway patrol aircraft."

Q: "And what happened, then, when you arrived in Oklahoma City?"

A: "We were met by the governor's limousine, we were driven

to the mansion, and we had dinner with the governor."

Q: "Mr. Mooney, when did you return, then, from Oklahoma City to Fort Worth?"

A: "We returned the following Monday approximately 10:00 a.m."

Q: "How did you travel back to Texas?"

A: "On the highway patrol aircraft."

Burkett then asked Mooney about what conversations he had with Taylor regarding his mansion visit.

D. C. Thomas was on his feet. "Your Honor, I'm going to object to that on the grounds that would be hearsay as to David Hall."

Judge Daugherty ruled against Thomas, then turned to the jury to instruct them in the matter of hearsay testimony in a conspiracy trial:

> Ladies and Gentlemen of the jury, with reference to the conspiracy charge,... if you find this conspiracy existed, then so long as the conspiracy was underway, what any co-conspirator said is binding on all you find to be co-conspirators, whether they were present or not... As far as the conspiracy count, if you find such a conspiracy, you may consider it.

The rule of law here is that hearsay--what one witness says that another person said--is generally not admissible in court; however, there are exceptions. One exception to the hearsay rule is that one member of a conspiracy can testify as to what other members of that same conspiracy said. That rule extends to any other witness to the conspiracy. Since Mooney had already pled guilty to a charge of conspiracy involving Hall and Taylor, he was thereby allowed to testify to the conversations with his alleged co-conspirators.

As it turned out, the argument over hearsay testimony was a tempest in a teapot. Mooney really didn't have much to say about that conversation--other than Hall wanted them to get together again.

Mooney was asked about their next meeting, which took place December 2 at Meacham Field in Fort Worth. He said that Hall told Taylor all about the Palo Mesa project, leaving Taylor only a few minutes to talk about his own plan. He said that Taylor had reduced the amount from $20 million to $10 million.

Again, Burkett asked, "How did the governor arrive in Fort Worth that day?"

"On the highway patrol aircraft."

Next came some of the most damning testimony thus far. "At the conclusion of the conversation," Mooney recounted, "the governor requested that I leave the room and walk down with him towards the aircraft."

Q: "What conversation did you have there?"

A: "He said that the purchase price of such a program... would be worth a finder's fee of approximately one percent and that he would like to earn 50 percent of the finder's fee."

Q: "What else did he say about that?"

A: "He asked that I notify Taylor that he felt the program was worth a one point finder's fee commission and asked me to find out if it was agreeable to him."

Q: "Did he say how he would receive his share of this?"

A: "He wanted to earn $12,500 a year, after leaving office, for a period of four years."

Mooney testified that he was stunned by the request for half the finder's fee. He returned to the office there at the airport and told Taylor that Hall wanted one percent of the $10 million, and that he was to receive half and "I was to receive the other half of a finder's fee."

Q: "What did Mr. Taylor say?"

A: "Mr. Taylor considered it. He had been accustomed, he told me, to paying finder's fees on such proposals and financial circulars in New York, the formula being five percent of the first million, four percent of the second million, three percent of the third million, two percent, one percent, which is a normal formula for finder's fees throughout the business world. So in view of that, Taylor considered it and said, well, one percent would be agreeable to him.''

The following day, according to Mooney, he received a phone call from Hall in which Hall asked if the one percent deal was agreeable to Taylor. Mooney said it was. Later that same day, he and Taylor received a phone call to appear at the meeting of the Oklahoma Retirement Fund the following day, which was December 4. He then launched into a description of their unsuccessful presentation to the retirement fund board and their follow-up meeting with John Rogers.

"And when did you next hear from David Hall?"

On the 9th or 10th of December, Mooney wasn't sure. Hall called to say he had become aware of a piece of property in Houston which he thought would be valuable to Mooney, and asked if he would go down, look it over, and see if it had any merit of purchase. He identified the property as being owned by Lynn [Buddy] Hall.

Mooney testified that in that same conversation, Hall mentioned he had offered Rogers half of the finder's fee, $25,000, to put across the program.

Q: "Did he tell you who was going to pay it?"

A: "He told me he expected me to share one half of the expense."

Q: "What was your reaction to that?"

A: "Well, I was chapped and I really didn't like it, and I was slightly shocked by it."

That was a damaging admission, inasmuch as that $25,000 figure directly corroborated what the prosecutors already knew would be John Rogers' later testimony. Also, the line of questioning made it clear that Hall didn't *ask* Mooney if he would pay, he *told* him that he would pay.

Mooney testified that he saw Doc Taylor on the 7th of December at Taylor's office, at which time Taylor gave Mooney a draft of a commitment letter which Rogers or somebody representing the retirement fund would have to sign. (Burkett then entered the letter into evidence.) On the 12th of December

Mooney took the letter to John Rogers' office.

Q: "What conversation did you have with John Rogers?"

A: "I told him it was a necessary step in the purchase of this program that we have a contract.... He told me at the time that he would need an attorney general's opinion."

Q: "What other conversation did you have with Mr. Rogers on that day?"

A: "Mr. Rogers asked me if I had been informed that he was a participant. He questioned me very slyly and quietly, 'Do you know that I had been -- I was going to receive half of David's $50,000'? And at that time I thought about it for a moment and I told him honestly, yes, I had been told and I did know that he was going to be paid."

Mooney testified that on the 18th of December, he and Taylor came back to Oklahoma City. They met with John Rogers. Taylor knew that Rogers wanted to be paid and was expecting to receive half of the finder's fee. Rogers talked explicitly about being paid in cash. According to Mooney's recollection, "Mr. Taylor said that if John Rogers was to be paid anything for his assistance as a part of the finder's fee, it would have to be listed in the offering circular... because of a Security Exchange Commission ruling. So if anything, he would have to be paid in a form such as acting as a consultant for him on other work [such as] finding locations for buildings and other construction activities."

Q: "Who suggested the payment be as a consultant or as a feasibility study, something like that?"

A: "Mr. Taylor."

Mooney testified that David Hall called him at his home on New Year's Eve and asked him to call back on a pay telephone. "He gave me a number to call him and I went to a pay phone and did call him," Mooney testified.

Q: "What conversation did you have with him?"

A: "At that time Mr. Hall told me he had received information to the effect that he was being set up by John Rogers. In fact, he was being framed by John Rogers."

During this conversation, Hall told Mooney that there was an

Oklahoma statute which specifically prevented the payment of funds to any official, and he cautioned Mooney that under no circumstances should he or Taylor pay any money to Rogers.

At the conclusion of Hall's call, Mooney testified, he quickly called Taylor and told him about this conversation. Taylor was quite shaken by this revelation, and he asked Mooney to come to his house on New Year's day to discuss the matter, which he did. They discussed the program and that, to the best of their knowledge, it had been accepted in good faith by the investment committee on its merits. He said they also discussed alternative ways to pay Rogers, such as making a contribution to Rogers' campaign fund or utilizing the services of Rogers' construction firm and overpaying him for the work.

Mooney testified that they then called David Hall that same day because he, Mooney, wanted Taylor to hear directly from Hall what he had said. This was at approximately 10:00 p.m. Hall asked them to go to a pay phone and call him from there. They went to a Pizza Inn a few blocks from Taylor's office. Mooney handed Taylor the receiver so he could hear. Hall reiterated his warning about the payment of money. Until then, Taylor had been willing to make the payment but now he was very much concerned about it.

The remainder of Mooney's testimony dealt with the events that led up to Mooney's arrest. He testified that Taylor had shown him a check for $31,250 drawn in his, Mooney's, behalf.

On cross-examination by Linn, Mooney stated that Taylor was an honest and honorable man, that he had never known him to do a dishonest thing, and that he was trying to find a legal way to pay John Rogers.

Kevin Mooney was an excellent witness for the prosecution. The defense never touched him on cross-examination.

The one question the defense never put to him was why, after the warning that they were being set up, Mooney and Taylor didn't just fold their tents and go somewhere else. After all, they were talking with the Attorney General of the State Oklahoma; if they were not involved in a criminal conspiracy, why wouldn't they say, "Hey, this guy's shaking us down?"

The future pattern of the trial was now set. A government witness is first led through his testimony by the prosecutor, who elicits the evidence in a series of tightly formulated questions. The defense lawyers may object to these questions if they believe the subject is outside the scope of the witness's knowledge, if the form of the question is not clear enough to provide a precise, factual answer, or if it might lead to speculation on the part of the witness.

Following the government's direct examination, each defendant may cross-examine the witness on the topics raised by the government. The lawyers are always called in the order of the indictment--Hall first, Taylor last.

Cross-examination is followed by redirect--if the government chooses--followed if necessary by recross, redirect, and so on until every last drop has been squeezed out.

The refereeing of these rules is a principle judicial function, and a measure of the judge's aptitude. In this case, Fred Daugherty's mind was logical, sharp, and uncluttered. He never lost the thread, and he seemed to work effortlessly. He was fully at ease in his robes.

A multi-defendant conspiracy trial like this one presented its own special problems, particularly for the defense. Often, the witness may give testimony about one defendant which has no relation whatsoever to the other man who is on trial. Almost always, it is in the best interest of the other defendant to lie low, say nothing, and maintain maximum distance.

The next government witnesses were five FBI agents: Paul Baresel, Jack DeWitt, Dwight Garretson, Ronald West, and Raymond Loll. Burkett led them through necessary but rather tedious testimony about how the tapes were recorded, had them identify each tape, and tell how the transcripts were made.

It was during their testimony that the defense lawyers

hammered away at the accuracy of the transcripts. That seemed to be their main concern--not the tapes themselves, but the written transcripts. There were numerous instances where the word "unintelligible" appeared, and a few instances in which two parties were talking at once. In at least one place, a comment was wrongly attributed to David Hall.

However, since the prosecution never planned to introduce the written transcripts into evidence anyway, it seemed that the defense was wasting its energy arguing against something that really wasn't worth arguing at all. The only thing the prosecutors had in mind was for the jury to have the transcripts before them while listening to the tapes.

§ § §

9

The Prosecution - Act II

The Courtroom. John Rogers was to be the prosecution's key witness. Burkett put him on next. His format was to have Rogers testify about a conversation, state that it was taped, and then play the tape for the jury. The plan was to proceed through the entire list of tapes in this fashion, *ad seriatim.*

The jury listened on earphones. The effect was devastating.

Initially, Rogers described the December 3 conversation with Governor Hall in the Blue Room at the capitol.

Q: "What conversation did you have at that time, Mr. Rogers?"

A: "The governor stated to me that this was no ordinary deal, that it was worth $50,000."

Q: "As nearly as possible, could you tell us what he said in his words."

A: "John, this is no ordinary deal. It is worth $50,000, 25 for you and 25 for me."

Ordinarily, the prosecution would have to rely on Rogers' credibility--his word against Hall's. But in this instance Mooney had already testified that Hall told him he had cut Rogers in for $25,000. That directly corroborated Rogers' testimony.

Q: "All right. What else did he say?"

A: "He told me to put the machinery in order to get it done."

Rogers was then asked to relate his immediate visit to Attorney

General Derryberry's office.

Q: "How did you leave the Blue Room, Mr. Rogers?"

A: "I went out the opposite end, the north entrance to the Blue Room, into the foyer, out the swinging doors, which lead into the treasurer's office, down the corridor, down the steps, around the back of the Rotunda to Larry Derryberry's office."

Rogers explained that he took the indirect route to Derryberry's office because he thought possibly the governor might be walking down the stairs on the opposite side and see him go around to the attorney general's office. Derryberry wasn't there, so Rogers returned to his own office. He testified that a fellow named Tom Jaworski happened to be in the foyer. Jaworski worked for the state legislature and his wife, Crystal, worked in Rogers' office. Rogers mentioned to Jaworski that the governor had just offered him a $25,000 bribe.

With regard to his consent to be taped, Rogers testified that, in fact, it was *his* idea to record the conversations, first proposing the idea to Attorney General Derryberry and then to the FBI.

Q: "What else did you tell them?"

A: "Well, towards the end of the meeting I consented to their operations of monitoring devices, to wear a transmitter,... to wear a body recorder and to allow them to wire my phones."

Q: "Were all of these recordings made with your consent?"

A: "Absolutely."

Q: "As a matter of fact, whose idea was it to record these conversations, Mr. Rogers?"

A: "My own."

Q: "And why did you do it?"

A: "I wanted to prove the one-on-one conversation wherein I was asked to be involved in an illegal and immoral situation and I wanted to prove myself."

Since the tapes were going to be the prosecution's best evidence, Burkett wanted the jury to hear the extreme care that Rogers and the FBI took to safeguard the authenticity of the recordings. Accordingly, he tracked Rogers through the procedures they followed in handling the tapes. (This might be termed CYA testimony.)

Q: "What did you do with the tapes of conversations made when an FBI agent was not present?"

A: "Nothing. I left them in the recorder."

Q: "And what did you do with the recorder then?"

A: "I delivered the recorder to the FBI on the way home, or to the office, whichever the occasion might be."

Q: "Did you ever remove a tape from the recorder?"

A: "No, sir."

Q: "Did you ever erase anything on any tape?"

A: "No, sir."

Q: "Did you ever splice any of the tapes?"

A: "No, sir."

Q: "Did you ever add anything to a tape after the conversation was over?"

A: "No, sir."

Q: "Did you ever make or try to make a copy of any of these tapes?"

A: "No, sir."

Q: "Did you ever change any of these tapes in any way?"

A: "Not in any way."

The first taped conversation took place on December 12. At this point, and after Rogers had testified only that he and Mooney had a conversation, Burkett offered the first tape into evidence. Judge Daugherty called the lawyers to the bench. "It seems to me," he said, "that when you get into these tapes, number one, the witness ought to testify what took place... and then it seems to me the next procedure would be for you to play the tapes."

Burkett said it didn't make any difference to him, except that it would shorten the trial considerably if they didn't have to go through the same material twice. The judge did not make a ruling, but he reiterated his thought that it would be better to have the witness say what happened, then back it up with a tape. Of course, Burkett deferred to his judgment.

It was at this point that the judge ruled against the motion to place the transcripts before the jury to follow along as they listened to the tapes. He said that the parties had not stipulated to their accuracy, and without a stipulation (agreement between the parties), the transcripts would merely reflect what the transcriber believed to have been said. At the same time, however, he indicated that he would have no objection to the prosecution's using the transcripts to argue before the jury; he just wasn't going to give them to the jury.

When they got through with the procedural matters and were ready to hear the December 12 tape, Burkett said, "Judge, this is an hour-and-a-half conversation." (He meant to suggest that the judge's proposed procedure was too time consuming.)

The judge quipped, "I don't care how long it is. I've got a lifetime job." (That struck Burkett as doubly funny because he got damned few humorous remarks from Fred Daugherty.)

The prosecution followed the same procedure with every tape: first Rogers would testify as to what took place, and then Agent DeWitt played the tape. That continued for the next three-and-a-half days as they worked through the tapes, one by one.

The taped conversation of December 18th was very important to the prosecution's case. Rogers testified that he went to the FBI office and was wired with a tape recorder and body mike. About noon that day Mooney and Taylor came to Rogers' office. Rogers immediately began talking about doing the deal at eight percent. They went to the Capitol cafeteria for lunch. Rogers said Hall had told him that at eight-and-a-quarter percent they would split $50,000, and he asked Taylor what they could expect at eight percent. Taylor said, "Well you understand, I can't pay you anything directly because I would have to show it in the prospectus, but we'd pay you for something else." Taylor said it would be worth an eighth of a point. Rogers said, "So you're saying that a quarter-of-a point [in interest] is worth an extra eighth of a point [finder's fee]?"

Q: "What, if anything, did Taylor say in that regard?" Burkett asked.

Rogers quoted Taylor as saying, "After we develop a paying

record, then we can lower the secure ladder a little bit and raise the rate or leave more room, you know, for the players.''

Q: "What, if anything was said, Mr. Rogers, about the schedule or timing of the payoff?''

A: "He said that when he was assured of its going through, that he would cut a check for half of the payoff, which would, at that time, be $31,250.''

According to Rogers, Taylor said he would like to pay him, if possible, in a manner having to do with "overpayment of some construction firm work or for feasibility studies on projects that were not to be completed... so that it couldn't be traced back to his paying me.''

That was very damaging testimony, of course, and the jury got to hear it all on tape.

It was now mid-afternoon. Recess.

During the recess, two reporters--Tony Clark of Channel 9 and Pam Henry of Channel 4--came to Burkett's office to get clarification as to what had been said on one of the tapes. (All those in front of the bar, including the jury, had earphones, but the press had to listen on loudspeakers in the spectators' section--and sometimes their reproduction was not of the highest quality.) Burkett showed them the written transcript of that conversation.

When court resumed at 4:20, Judge Daugherty called the lawyers to the bench for a sidebar conference at the request of D. C. Thomas.

The side bar is the side of the bench farthest away from the jury. The judge and lawyers can confer there without risk of being overheard, and it is easier to whisper at the bench than to send fourteen people out of the room. All lawyers, prosecution and defense, have a right to listen in on the sidebars, as such conferences are called.

Thomas moved for a mistrial. "During the recess we just had, the United States Attorney did exhibit to members of the press, to wit, Pam Henry and Tony Clark, copies of the transcripts.'' Thomas said this deprived Hall of his rights to due process and to a fair and impartial trial.

"How has this had anything to do with the trial?" Daugherty asked.

Thomas suggested that the jury would read the papers. "They've been instructed not to read the papers," the judge replied.

Thomas persisted, "Well, what if they do?" The judge replied, "I have to assume that they will follow my instructions, there's a presumption that they will do so."

Thomas also asked the court to instruct Jack Dewitt, the FBI agent, not to touch the controls after the tape started playing, but the judge said he had been watching Dewitt, and when the tape began to fade he turned the sound up, and that was okay.

All the motions made by Hall's attorney were overruled. Jimmy Linn made no motions on behalf of Taylor at this time.

...Thursday, February 27, 1975
The Courtroom.   John Rogers was still on the witness stand. He described the tape of December 19 in which he called David Hall and told him that the First National Bank was going to write a negative letter "unless somebody put the strongarm on them." Hall told him he was going to call Leo Winters, the State Treasurer, and have him pressure the bank. Rogers said that Taylor and Mooney should pay him "half when we got the paperwork done and half was to be paid when the deal went through," and Hall said, "That's right." That was very incriminating.

The tape was then played for the jury. This was a pretty good quality recording.

The next tape was a telephone conversation that took place between Rogers and Hall on December 26. Rogers testified that Hall said that Leo Winters didn't want to go to the bank. Rogers then started talking about the payoff, but Hall said, "Don't talk to me about that."

The tape of January 3rd precipitated a ridiculous exchange between the attorneys. It was not a great moment for the court.

When the tape was over, D. C. Thomas said, "There's more to that tape, isn't there?"

BURKETT: "Oh, yes, there was."

THOMAS: "Your Honor, I object--"

THE COURT: "If you want to talk about it, we will talk up here. It's time for a recess at this time.

BURKETT: "Your Honor, there is a bit more sound on that tape."

THOMAS: "There certainly is."

BURKETT: "Do you want to do it before or after lunch?"

THE COURT: "It's just one sentence, we can do it now."

[A PORTION OF THE TAPE WAS PLAYED IN OPEN COURT IN THE PRESENCE AND HEARING OF THE JURY]

THOMAS: "Have them turn it up where I can hear what was said. I couldn't hear what was said."

THE COURT: "Neither could I."

[A PORTION OF THE TAPE WAS PLAYED AGAIN]

THOMAS: "I still can't understand it, Judge."

THE COURT: "Was it those several words that you're concerned about?"

THOMAS: "Yes. They are after he hangs up the telephone."

THE COURT: "Well, I heard some of the words, but I couldn't understand them."

DeWITT: "I'll try to turn it up louder, Your Honor."

THE COURT: "Try it once more."

[A PORTION OF THE TAPE WAS PLAYED AGAIN]

THE COURT: "I heard the words but I can't understand them. Perhaps you gentlemen can agree what the words are, if you want to, and tell the jury."

The court recessed until two o'clock.

After lunch, Burkett asked John Rogers, "Now you recall that after the conversation was over, Mr. Thomas asked about some faint words at the end of the tape, do you know what those words were?"

A: "Yes sir, I do."

Q: "Do you know who spoke them?"
A: "Yes sir, I do."
Q: "What were the words?"
A: "That's your best performance, John."
Q: "And who said that, Mr. Rogers?"
A: "FBI Agent Jack DeWitt."

Thomas's little *faux pas* backfired on him because it allowed the prosecution to bring out an important point that Burkett was anxious for the jury to understand, namely, that John Rogers was playing a part. Rogers said it well: "I was playing the role of a corrupt politician, I was playing a part - that was part of my role." The prosecution welcomed this opportunity to emphasize Rogers' role playing.

Jimmy Linn looked like he could have killed Thomas for making such a big deal about those words, because Linn was working hard to cast Rogers as a liar. "That was a lie wasn't it, Mr. Rogers?" he had shouted during the pre-trial hearing when Rogers told Taylor he was calling from his girlfriend's house when it was actually from FBI Agent Baresel's bedroom. The prosecution, of course, was doing just the opposite--trying to show it was a part of the act. This last little colloquy reinforced the prosecution's position very well.

The rest of Rogers' testimony was not spectacular at all. Mostly, it followed the same pattern--describe the conversation, then play the tape; describe the conversation, then play the tape. Ultimately, it was the tapes that proved to be the prosecution's star witness. There was no getting around what was being said; and the cumulative effect of listening to all that "plotting, planning, and conspiring" was devastating for the defense.

...Friday, February 28, 1975
The Courtroom.   On this, his third day of direct examination, John Rogers continued to methodically track through his conversations with Hall, Taylor and Mooney, testifying to what each had said, and then the tapes were played for the jury.

The evidence continued to mount.

...Monday, March 3, 1975

The Courtroom.   The direct testimony of Rogers ended with the playing of the last tape containing two short conversations, one with W. W. Taylor on January 13 and the other with Kevin Mooney on January 14.

The Taylor conversation took place over the telephone when Taylor was in Jackson, Mississippi. Rogers said, "Doc, I give up! Come get the letter."

The Mooney conversation took place the following day in Rogers' office when Mooney came to pick up the commitment letter, and was arrested. Clearly audible on the tape were the words, "I am Ted Rosack, FBI, you're under arrest and I'll take the letter."

Finally, Burkett wanted John Rogers to explain to the jury his use of intemperate language on some of the tapes, even though he knew he was being taped.

Q: "Mr. Rogers, why did you do that?"

A: "I was playing the part of a corrupt politician. I do use vulgar language, I'm not saying that I don't. Something that I've tried to correct since my Marine Corps days but I was expressly trying to look like the trash they thought I was, the corrupt politician."

Q: "You also made some derogatory comments about Governor Boren and about Attorney General Derryberry, why did you do that?"

A: "I did that expressly because I knew them to be David Hall's political enemies. Governor Boren had just defeated him, Larry Derryberry had tried to have an investigation, and an unsuccessful one; I knew they were his enemies and I was playing the part."

The defense's only hope of neutralizing John Rogers' testimony was to throw out the tapes. The only way they could do that was to convince the jury that the consent to these recordings given by

John Rogers was coerced by the government. If the consent was coerced, then the judge would tell the jury to disregard the tape recordings. On the other hand, if the jury found that the consent was not coerced but freely and voluntarily given by Rogers, then they may consider the recordings. So, essentially, the only question was whether or not Rogers was coerced on or about December 9, 1974, to engage in electronic surveillance.

Jimmy Linn began the cross-examination with a blistering attack on Rogers' credibility. Linn implied that Rogers was afraid that Larry Derryberry might prosecute him or use the information Rogers had given him about the bribe to further his own political ambitions. He tried to imply that Rogers was worried that he might be prosecuted for pleading his Fifth Amendment rights before the grand jury. This was denied, of course, and Linn knew better--that a citizen cannot be prosecuted for taking the Fifth--but he sought to plant a seed in the jury's mind anyway.

Linn sought to impeach Rogers on the basis of former testimony, the testimony he'd given at the February 7 evidentiary hearing. The judge explained to the jury:

> Impeaching a witness [is] showing that on a prior occasion he has made a statement, either under oath or otherwise, contrary to testimony given here in open court.

Linn had gone through Rogers' testimony and tried to find every deviation, every inconsistency, he could find in it. He would read Rogers a portion of what he'd said back on February 7, and then ask, "Didn't you testify to this or that?" Time and again, Burkett would object that what Rogers said today wasn't substantially different from what he had said then. Judge Daugherty would say, "I agree," and sustain the objection.

That happened so often that Jimmy Linn approached the bench to complain, "Judge, I really wish you wouldn't agree with Mr. Burkett that I'm not contradicting this man from time to time."

Daugherty rebuffed him. "Well, your questions have not been completely proper on the impeaching angle.... A lot of the things you've been reading are not really inconsistent with his reading of them. If they are, let him explain them."

Linn took the ruling with good grace, "If the court is not going to do that, I wish he would, on the other side, say 'You got him there.'"

"No, it doesn't work that way," quipped the judge.

Linn then took Rogers back to a 1967 Securities and Exchange Commission (SEC) action brought against Rogers and other investors. Burkett objected because it was irrelevant. Linn argued that he was presenting it for two reasons; one, because it went to the issue of whether or not Rogers' consent to the taping was coerced, and second, the SEC had enjoined Rogers from selling certain stock--yet on one of the tapes Rogers mentioned this stock was for sale to Taylor. Linn tried to imply that Rogers was intending to do something illegal. Burkett contended that Rogers was merely play-acting a role and had no intention of selling the stock. The judge agreed.

Jimmy Linn then hammered away at a non-prosecution letter Burkett had written Rogers in December, implying that it was a trade-off to get his consent to making the tapes, hence coercion. This was a matter related to an independent investigation into the transfer of campaign funds from the war chest of Rogers' dad, John M. Rogers, into the David Hall campaign. Rogers had "taken the Fifth" when the grand jury asked him about this. Rogers realized this was a mistake politically, and Burkett told him if he would make a full disclosure about the campaign fund--which he did, then the government would not prosecute. Then followed the letter. Unfortunately, the timing of the letter--December 23--made it look like it was connected to this case. Jimmy Linn tried to characterize it as a letter of immunity.

Q: "Now, that concern [about being prosecuted] was alleviated a little bit later, like the 23rd of December, when you were granted immunity from prosecution, was it not?"

A: "I have not been granted immunity now, then, or ever. I asked for nothing when I went to see Mr. Burkett."

Linn opened a can of worms when, a little later, he asked

Rogers if he ever consulted anybody as to the political consequences of doing this undercover work.

Rogers replied, "I may have talked about political consequences having to do with helping to prove David Hall was a crook, but I wouldn't have--"

The word "crook" brought D. C. Thomas to his feet in a flash, "I object Your Honor!" Approaching the bench, he asked for a mistrial, saying, "the word 'crook' was used for the sole and obvious purpose of biasing and prejudicing this jury..."

Judge Daugherty's response was a succinct: "That's the witness' language and apparently his opinion. He felt that's what he was about to do, or a crime connected with this case.... After all the language we've heard, that's a rather mild word."

The motion for mistrial was overruled, and the court adjourned for lunch.

When court resumed after its lunch break, another tempest was brewing--and another motion for mistrial to be addressed. The judge called the lawyers to the bench and showed them a letter he had received from Tony Clark, a newscaster from KWTV Channel 9 in Oklahoma City. Clark said he had called three of the jurors in this case in an effort to get some background information on them, primarily their ages, and he explained to them that he knew they were not to discuss the case--nor did he want to discuss the case with them. He said one juror's mother answered the phone and told him how old the juror was, but the other two jurors declined to talk to him.

Daugherty didn't seem particularly concerned, indicating, "I intend to file it with the Clerk as the Court's Exhibit, for whatever it's worth."

Similarly, Burkett said, "Your Honor, I have read the letter and have no desires about it one way or the other. I don't think it involves any error or any prejudice."

Jimmy Linn observed laconically, "Looks like a nice letter, Judge." Apparently, he wasn't upset about it either.

But D. C. Thomas was outraged. Or at least, he appeared to be.

He wanted the judge to call Clark in and put him under oath so that he could question him about it.

"You have a right to do that on your own," the judge said. "If you want to talk to him, go talk to him."

"I want it on the record under oath," Thomas insisted.

The judge forcefully iterated his opinion to Thomas: "I can't see that he's done anything except been overzealous and improper in calling the jury for any reason. He laid it on the line. If you want to find out what he said in the letter, why, you're free to go ahead and do it."

Then he went on to express his own frustration--and probably that of many fellow judges--with the news media:

"I don't appreciate what he's done, but those of us who have to live with the news media know the news media is unmanageable, uncontrollable, and aggressive. They make mistakes, as you well know. I would just as soon we didn't have to fool with [them] in the trial. They are nothing but a headache as far as I am concerned. This is just another example of it. But I don't think there's any jury damage based on this letter."

Linn wound up his cross-examination by trying to get Rogers to say that Taylor's plan was a good plan. Rogers would only go so far as to acknowledge that it might be a "good plan for some type of investors, but not for our fund."

On his cross-examination, D. C. Thomas went directly to the meeting in the Blue Room on December 3. He asked Rogers if he had recorded any tapes which contained a discussion of the meeting in the Blue Room.

A: "I'm not sure. I thought I did."

Q: "Are you telling the ladies and gentlemen of the jury that on these tapes, on any telephone call that you had with David Hall on those tapes, that you mentioned a conference in the Blue Room or a bribe in the Blue Room or conversation in the Blue Room?"

A: "I would prefer to let the tapes speak for themselves."

The funny thing about this colloquy was that, after all of the hullabaloo the lawyers went through about whether or not the jury should be allowed to see the written transcripts, D. C. Thomas himself held in his hand a copy of the forbidden transcript throughout his intense grilling of Rogers. It seemed to Burkett that this act served only to validate the prosecution's best evidencee.

Thomas questioned Rogers at length about his conversation with Hall on December 18. He noted that as of that date, Hall didn't know who all the board members were and Rogers had to give him the list over the phone. In effect, he was he was trying to show that Hall wasn't responsible for any of these actions.

After finishing this line of questioning, Thomas asked Rogers to step over to the exhibit that was a layout of the Blue Room and put an "X" on the spot where he had stood during one of the conversations with the governor. Burkett was puzzled. Possibly this was because Thomas later planned to call a rebuttal witness.

Then, with a dramatic flourish, Thomas produced a piece of paper, wrote a date on it, handed it to Rogers and asked, "What is the date written on that piece of paper?"

A: "November 8, 1974."

Q: "All right, sir. I'm going to put that piece of paper in that envelope and I'm going to seal it in your presence. Mr. Rogers, my last question will be, would you put your initials on that sealed envelope for me?"

Rogers did, and Thomas put the envelope away, leaving the prosecution--and the jury--to wonder what the mystery was about.

On re-direct, Burkett referred to the IRS and SEC investigations. He asked John Rogers specifically if any of those investigations had any impact on his consent to make the tapes. His answer was, "No."

Burkett shored up a couple of other minor details. Neither Jimmy Linn nor D. C. Thomas were able to score any points on their re-cross. Rogers was excused.

John Rogers had been on the witness stand the better part of five days. He made an excellent witness.

§ § §

10

The Prosecution- Act III

...Monday, March 3, 1975
The Courtroom.   The conclusion of John Rogers' testimony meant the case for the prosecution was pretty well wrapped up. All that remained was to tidy up some loose ends. The remaining witnesses were called mainly to provide corroborating testimony.

The next witness was Irene Messick, executive secretary for Attorney General Larry Derryberry. She was on very briefly. Ms. Messick testified that John Rogers came to the attorney general's office on December 4 and asked to see Derryberry. It was 9:30 in the morning. Rogers told her it was very important that he see Mr. Derryberry as soon as possible. She described him as "very fidgety, just walked back and forth in front of my desk."

On cross-examination, both Thomas and Linn had her go into the procedures for determining what things she put in the log and what she didn't. In so doing, they merely emphasized what had happened.

That is a common occurrence in the courtroom, namely, that lawyers seem to think they *have* to cross-examine every witness. According to Bill Burkett, a "no questions" response is sometimes a lot better because it's not your witness--it's a *hostile* witness--and you want to avoid giving them a chance to tell their story again.

The day ended with Larry Derryberry, the state attorney

general, on the stand. He testified as to his role in the investigation. He said that he came into his office at 11:30 the morning of December 4th and returned a call to John Rogers, but Rogers was not in. He saw Rogers around 4:00 or 4:30 that afternoon, and they went to the office of the Chief of the Criminal Division of the AG's office and talked. As a result of that conversation, he called Ted Rosack of the FBI the next day and told him that he had information from an informant that he needed to discuss. He also called Tom Puckett, who was assistant chief of the Oklahoma State Bureau of Investigation (OSBI).

Derryberry testified that Puckett came to his office, and he told Puckett that an informant had been offered a $25,000 bribe by Governor Hall and asked if the OSBI could investigate this. He did not tell Puckett who the informant was, because he did not want to compromise Puckett, who was under the governor. The following Monday, he learned from Puckett that it would be difficult for the OSBI to handle the investigation. After assuring Rogers that the FBI could be trusted, Derryberry said he called Ted Rosack and went to Rosack's office, taking Puckett with him.

He described the meeting in the FBI office where plans were made for Rogers to do the taping. He said he told the group that Rogers was the best person to do the undercover work because he was "extremely brash, almost to the point of arrogance, and that he had the guts to see it through."

...Tuesday, March 4, 1975

The Courtroom.   This snowy, soggy morning began with Larry Derryberry in the witness box and D. C. Thomas conducting the cross-examination.

Thomas delved into the 1973 indictment of State Treasurer Leo Winters. Winters had a scheme whereby he would put a million dollars of state funds, interest free, into a bank that agreed to pay him $250 a month. Winters didn't use that money personally; rather, he used it to contribute to various political campaigns around the state. He fancied himself as a "kingmaker," so to speak. Larry Derryberry was a beneficiary of those funds.

At the time of Winters' indictment, Burkett was quoted in the newspapers as saying, "The grand jury felt that Mr. Derryberry had no way of knowing that the money was illegally obtained." D. C. Thomas tried to play up that incident to embarrass Derryberry and to imply that Derryberry was falsifying his testimony to repay Burkett.

Thomas asked, "The paper called you the mystery candidate, didn't they?"

A: "Well, they may have called me that but I don't think there was any mystery about it."

Q: "Well, the indictment said 'Unnamed,' didn't it?"

A: "Yes, that's correct."

Q: "Mr. Burkett pursued, is that correct?"

A: "Yes, sir, that's correct."

Q: "Had to do with a bank here in town which paid an agency some $500 for a car for you to drive around during your 1970 campaign, is that right?"

A: "Yes, sir."

Q: "And a money and stamps type of procedure whereby they rented an apartment in which you lived."

A: "That's correct."

Q: "Did it ever occur to you, Mr. Derryberry, to ask somebody who was paying your rent where you were living and who was paying for your car that you were driving?"

At that point, Burkett rose to object, "Excuse me just a minute, Your Honor. I'm perfectly willing to enter all of this--"

The judge cut in, "Just make an objection, if you have one!"

"Well, I just want to make sure, Your Honor, if we have to go over all of it. This is irrelevant and immaterial, and--"

"I think it's irrelevant," Daugherty replied.

The judge's response caught Burkett in mid sentence, "--on his part to raise a point that he thinks is embarrassing to Mr. Derryberry--"

The judge moved to cut Burkett off: "I'm waiting for you to finish what supposedly is an objection, if you will just make it."

Burkett's point had already been made with the jury. "On

second thought," he said, "I don't believe I care to object, Your Honor. I believe I'll just withdraw it."

Then Daugherty took it upon himself to say, "I think I'll object because it's not material to the issues. The only purpose of allowing any of this testimony is to show this witness' possible interest in this litigation. It isn't appropriate to go into all the details of it. It's another matter that's too foreign from the lawsuit to go into the details. I think you've gone into it as far as I should permit, Mr. Thomas."

Nevertheless, D. C. Thomas persisted in his line of questioning, provoking another lecture from the judge. "I think you brought out this relationship, the press release, what it was about, in sufficient detail that you may now move on to something else."

"May I inquire into this witness's frame of mind?" Thomas asked.

"It's not his frame of mind that's important, it's the relationship of the two," ruled Daugherty.

After some more verbal jousting with the judge, Thomas finally gave up this attack and moved on to other issues.

Jimmy Linn re-crossed. It didn't go anywhere. Somewhat ironically, during Linn's re-cross, Judge Daugherty himself referred to a transcript of the tapes--which he had previously disallowed--to make a ruling from the bench.

Next up were four trustees of the Oklahoma Public Employees Retirement System. In order of appearance they were L. P. Williams, Jim Cook, Richard Ward, and J. L. Merrill. In each case, they testified that the governor had called them and told them he thought that Taylor's plan was a good one for Oklahoma. They said that the governor didn't apply overt pressure; however, each confirmed that the Governor had never contacted them previously about any matter coming before the board.

Doris Rogers, Max Stange's assistant, was next up. She testified that on November 6, 1974, she got a call from somebody at the governor's office wanting to make an appointment for W. W.

Taylor with Mr. Stange. The appointment was set for November 8, and on that day Mr. Taylor and another man met with Mr. Stange very briefly.

Max Stange, Director of OPERS, took the stand. Stange testified that Mr. Taylor and a Mr. Finlay came to see him on November 8, that he only talked to them for 15 or 20 minutes, and that it was a $20 million, 20-year proposal to borrow money from OPERS at 10.5 percent interest. He told them that they needed to talk to the chairman because he didn't have anything to do with investments, he just ran the office. He testified that he attended the November 13 meeting of the investment committee at which this deal was discussed after the regular business was concluded; that nobody expressed any interest, and Rogers threw it in the wastebasket.

He testified about the meetings on the 4th, 20th, and 23rd of December. Mooney called him on the 3rd of January and wanted a letter from the board agreeing to the deal. He said that on the 10th of January, Mooney brought in a proposal and asked for a letter authorizing the deal, and Stange declined to give it to him, saying he didn't have authority to do that.

Diane Gay, Doc Taylor's secretary, was called. She testified that on the 30th of December she was instructed by Taylor to write a check to Kevin Mooney for $31,250. She did so, and she stubbed it: "For legal services."

The only question asked her on cross-examination was by Jimmy Linn: "Mrs. Gay have you ever worked for a finer man than W. W. Taylor?" She got in her "No, sir" before the prosecution could object, although the objection was sustained.

Up next was Jim Duckels, Taylor's son-in-law. He testified that on the 30th of December, Diane Gay told him about the check for $31,250 to Kevin Mooney. Then on the 15th of January, when Taylor returned from Jackson, Mississippi, where he had been arrested, he (Duckels) and Taylor went out to the backyard swimming pool. He said Taylor told him, "Now I tore up the check, I never signed it. Go down there and change the endorsement so that unauthorized people could not see it."

Duckels testified that he went to Taylor's office and changed the check stub. He testified that Emmett Colvin, Taylor's Dallas lawyer, told him to change the check stub back. So on Colvin's instructions, he wrote across the stub: "This check originally payable to R. Kevin Mooney for $31,250."

Carroll Johnson from the First National Bank took the stand to testify that he never recommended the plan to the board but didn't tell the board or Taylor that his refusal was due to the U.S. Attorney asking them not to. Linn's cross-examination tried to get Johnson to say this was really a good plan, but Johnson wouldn't agree.

Court adjourned for the day until 9:30 a.m. the next morning.

The Judge's Chambers.

The continuing saga of Tony Clark still dogged the court. At D. C. Thomas's request, the judge called the lawyers into his chambers for round two of that hapless journalist's boo-boo in contacting jurors. Judge Daugherty didn't seem terribly enthusiastic about the idea; rather, it appeared to be another instance of his accommodating the defense so as to avoid giving them possible basis for an appeal.

D. C. did the questioning. He asked Clark to describe what happened.

Clark said the first phone call was to Priscilla Doss, around 7:30 or 8:00 on Friday evening. "A lady answered, and I said, 'Mrs. Doss?' And she said, 'Yes.' I said, 'My name is Tony Clark. I'm a television reporter from KWTV. I'm covering the Hall trial. I know that you're admonished not to talk about the Hall trial. I do not want to talk to you about the Hall trial. With your permission, I would like to find out your age.' At that time she said her age was 50, which somewhat surprised me because the young lady sitting on the jury is substantially younger. I said, 'Now, am I speaking to the lady who is the juror?' She said, 'No. That is my daughter, she's 25.' At that point I said 'Thank you,' and ended the conversation.''

He said the second and third phone calls were to Albert
LaMonte and Lillie Knox. In both instances, the juror declined to
talk. Clark said "Thank you," and ended the conversation. He
said he made no attempt to contact any other jurors. Clark said it
was on his own initiative that he felt a responsibility to inform the
judge as to what he had done.

Neither Jimmy Linn nor Burkett had any questions. A
chastened Tony Clark was excused. Clark never did explain why
he wanted to know their ages. The whole episode turned out to be
much ado about nothing.

...Wednesday, March 5, 1975

The Courtroom.   The prosecution's case was nearing its end.
Only a few more witnesses remained.

Starting off the morning was Tom Norwood, another officer
from First National Bank. His testimony mainly corroborated that
of Carroll Johnson from the day before.

Mac McGuire of Southwestern Bell Telephone Security
identified various telephone records of the governor and the
Centrex Board at the State Capitol building. He also identified
other telephone numbers as being located at pay phones at the
Pizza Inn, the Conoco station at N.W Highway and Pennsylvania,
and a Champlain station at N.W. Highway at Pennsylvania. There
was no cross-examination of him.

Ollie Joe Hazen, Centrex supervisor at the State Capitol,
identified various telephone numbers as being in the governor's
office. There was no cross-examination of her.

The prosecution brought in Jerry Wallace of Southwestern Bell
in Dallas, who likewise identified various telephone numbers and
records. He identified Taylor's home and office phones, pay
phones at the French Market Mall and at Jamie's Food Store.
These records corroborated the testimony of Mooney who had
said that when they talked to Hall, he would always tell them to
go to a pay phone and call him from there. The U.S. Attorney had
the records of those calls.

The final figure in the prosecution's parade of witnesses was

Lawrence Kirk, the highway patrol pilot assigned to the governor. He testified that he saw Hall and Mooney at Meacham Field in Fort Worth on the 30th of November; that he went to Love Field on the third of November and picked up Mooney and Taylor and brought them up to Oklahoma City; that he left Wiley Post on the second of December going to Meacham Field where he saw Hall meeting with Taylor and Mooney and that they were looking at "some type of chart or what looked like maybe an architectural drawing;" and that when they left Mooney walked out to the plane with Hall, although he couldn't hear their conversation.

Jim Duckels returned to the stand for a brief bit of cross-examination, in which he testified that Taylor told him Rogers was shaking him down and that he might abandon the deal. The judge allowed this testimony, he said, "...not to show the truth of the statement, but to show the state of mind of Taylor." This distinction seemed to be entirely lost on the jury.

The trial was about to enter a new phase. After presenting 24 witnesses and more than seven days of evidence, the government was finally concluding its case-in-chief. Now would be the defense's turn. What would their strategy be? Dangerous games were in high gear.

After the jury retired, Judge Daugherty called the lawyers to the bench to handle a few procedural motions, one of which was to announce his ruling that the three taped conversations between Dorothy Pike and David Hall were legal, but had no relevance to this case. During some wrangling over one of the finer points of law, Bill Burkett was momentarily heartened when Jimmy Linn said, "Judge, I trust what Mr. Burkett says...," but then Linn dropped the other shoe, "...except when he's announcing the law."

§ § §

11

The Defense - Hall

The Courtroom.   For four years the state's First Lady, the attractive, raven-haired Jo Evans Hall, had become a familiar figure to the spectators who daily packed the courtroom for the unfolding drama. Seated in the first row on the defense side, directly behind her husband, she leaned forward from time to time to signal him encouragement. If she was worried about the trial's outcome, it certainly did not show on her attractive features; she never failed to exhibit poise and character.

The pair met on a blind date in December 1955 while David was in law school and Jo was a stewardess for American Airlines. Mrs. Hall grew up in the small rural town of Morrilton, Arkansas, and after graduating from college she trained as a stewardess. She stayed with the airline for two more years while her husband completed his law degree. Their three children were named Nancy Leigh, Douglas David, and Julie Beth.

One-thirty p.m. The jury was in the box. Judge Daugherty took a moment to announce, "Ladies and Gentlemen of the jury, you heard the evidence presented to you by the government-in-chief. Defendant Hall reserved his [opening statement], which is a permissible and customary procedure in a criminal-type case. At this time you will hear the opening statement presented to you by counsel for the defendant Hall."

D. C. Thomas strode to the podium, looked at each of the jurors piercingly, and solemnly began, "If the Court please, Ladies and

Gentlemen of the jury, the evidence of David Hall will show that he didn't do it."

The court waited expectantly, lawyers and spectators alike. They expected him to continue with a spirited statement. But he did not. That was it. Undoubtedly, this was one of the shortest opening statements ever uttered in a court of law. *Ladies and Gentlemen of the jury, the evidence of David Hall will show that he didn't do it.*"[1]

The next words from Thomas' mouth were, "Your Honor, for my first witness, I call Robert Sanders."

Robert Sanders was the fellow from Florida who came through Oklahoma City at Christmas-time and dropped in on John Rogers to renew an old acquaintance. Sanders testified that he was a political consultant who had previously done polling in Oklahoma and now was county administrator of Leon County, Tallahassee, Florida. He said Rogers asked for his expert opinion on what would be the impact on Rogers' political image when the news broke of his role in the Hall investigation.

Sanders testified that later, he "decided for better or for worse, I would pass it on to David." Hall returned the call while Sanders was at dinner in Jamil's Restaurant on Lincoln Boulevard. Sanders took it in the restaurant kitchen. Sanders said he related to Hall what Rogers had told him, then advised the governor, "It's set up for you to pay the money to John on the 31st of December, New Year's Eve." According to Sanders, Hall professed to be shocked.

On cross-examination, Burkett asked, "Did [Rogers] mention that he was working with the Federal Bureau of Investigation, undercover?"

A: "He mentioned the FBI, yes, sir."

Q: "Did he mention that the attorney general of this state was also helping direct the undercover activities?"

A: "Yes, sir."

Q: "Did you consider that your action in advising the governor of this might amount to obstruction of justice?"

Over strong objections by Thomas and Linn, Judge Daugherty

directed Sanders to answer the question.

A: "No, sir,... it had never occurred to me that there was any truth to what John Rogers said."

That, of course, was ludicrous. If Sanders didn't believe it to be true, why did he bother calling Hall?

As a matter of fact, Burkett never understood why Thomas put Sanders on the stand; his testimony only hurt Hall. Perhaps D. C. was merely using everything he had in his arsenal in hopes that somehow it might be helpful.

Thomas' next witness was Richard Wiseman, a highway patrolman who was assigned to the governor's office for security. Direct examination was conducted by Jack Dawson. Wiseman testified a log book was maintained of whom the governor met with and whom he saw. Moreover, there were TV cameras strategically placed around the office suite. He testified that he was on duty from 8:00 a.m. until 3:00 p.m. on December 3, 1974, and he never saw the governor leave to go see John Rogers in the Blue Room. That was the essence of his testimony

Then came Robert D. Simms, Supreme Court Justice, who testified as a character witness. Simms testified that he hired David Hall as an assistant district attorney in Tulsa in 1958, and that Hall succeeded him as district attorney when he, Simms, left to become a district judge. He stated that Hall had a reputation for being an honest, law-abiding citizen. There was no cross examination.

Generally, character witnesses have limited value. They can testify that they are familiar with the defendant's reputation for truth and veracity and that his reputation is good. That's it. They're not even allowed to give examples. Obviously, the defense strategy was to get important people as character witnesses, or persons with whom they think the jury might be impressed.

Burkett rarely cross-examined a character witness. This trial was no exception

D. C. Thomas sought to score some points with a witness named Jon Randolf Floyd, an employee of the Department of State. Floyd testified that on November 8 he had lunch with Crystal Jaworski, an employee in John Rogers' office. Afterward he went to the mansion and told Jo Hall, the governor's wife, that there was a possibility that John Rogers was getting ready to set up David.

On cross examination, Floyd acknowledged that he hadn't contacted D. C. Thomas about this matter until shortly before the trial started. He also claimed that the U.S. Attorney had been in touch with John Rogers and put him under some kind of pressure. In point of fact, Burkett had never even met John Rogers until November 27, and Rogers' remark to Crystal Jaworski's husband didn't occur until December 3.

The defense tried to show there was a conspiracy set up to trap David Hall. The fact that they didn't have any evidence to support it didn't deter Thomas from trying, however, because that was the only defense he could put up. The problem they faced was how to overcome the weight of all those tapes in which Hall and Taylor were saying very incriminating things--things that were very difficult to explain. So, really, he was just trying to make something out of nothing.

Frank McDivitt, 42, a tax attorney of engaging modesty, had been Governor Hall's personal lawyer in the suits involving the whereabouts of Dorothy Pike. He now came to the witness stand in defense of his client.

McDivitt testified that on November 8th he received a telephone call from the governor's wife, Jo Hall, in which she asked him to meet with her at the Mansion.

Q: "What was the subject matter of your visit with Mrs. Hall?"
A: "John Rogers, Jr."

Thomas did not follow up with any questions about the content of that conversation, nor a subsequent November 19 conversation he had with David Hall upon the latter's return.

Nor did Burkett. Rather, his cross examination focused on the

several lawsuits McDivitt had filed in Hall's behalf, including one
against the phone company for allegedly tapping his lines.

"Did you win any of them?" Burkett asked.

He squirmed. "Well,... there are still two pending."

In short, Hall didn't win any of them. The only thing
McDivitt's testimony did was to plant in the jury's mind the idea
that *something* began on November 8 that suggested a conspiracy
to "get" the governor. He provided no substantive information
whatever.

The day ended with another character witness on the stand, a
woman named Beulah Pless, who had been superintendent of the
Oklahoma County Home. She said Hall had been the only
governor in 50 years to visit the county poor farm.

...Thursday, March 6, 1975

The Courtroom.   Ed Hardy, the governor's press secretary, was
the lead-off witness for the day. Burkett couldn't imagine why on
earth they called him; his testimony only corroborated the
government's case.

Hardy testified that he had free access to the governor's office,
and on an afternoon early in January--he couldn't remember the
exact date--he saw a note in plain view on the governor's desk,
written in David Hall's handwriting. The note said, "We are
bugged." He said he wadded it up and threw it into the
wastebasket.

On cross examination, Hardy testified that the frequency of the
visits between David Hall and John Rogers increased in the time
frame of December of 1974 to January of 1975.

Q: "Did you notice, in December and January, the frequency of
[Rogers] visits with the Governor increased?"

A: "I certainly did."

Q: "You noticed that, did you not?"

A: "Yes, I did."

Four more character witnesses paraded quickly on and off the stand. First was State Senator E. Melvin Porter, who himself was quite a character. He was followed by Lorenz Huenemann, pastor of South Minister Presbyterian Church in Tulsa, where David Hall was a member. Then there was Rose Marie Lipe, assistant corporate secretary of Oklahoma Natural Gas, who was a friend and neighbor. Last was Robert L. Anderson, chairman of the science department of Putnam City High School. All testified that David Hall had a reputation for being truthful and honest.

Tension and nervous energy were evident everywhere. Tall, bulky, silvery-maned David Hall strode to the witness box, outwardly as confident and self-assured as he had ever been.

Q: "Would you state your name to the Court and the jury."

A: "My name is David Hall."

Q: "Governor, when is the first time you ever met Kevin Mooney?"

A: "When we were both students at the University of Tulsa School of Law."

Q: "When and where did yourself and Kevin Mooney first discuss an employees' retirement investment fund?"

A: "The first mention of that was at Meacham Field in the office of Don Hanson."

Hall described the conversation as being very brief. He said that Mooney stated he knew of a plan that would be good for the state of Oklahoma and asked if Hall would like to look at the plan. Hall said he would, and he sent the highway patrol plane to Dallas to pick up Mooney and Taylor for a dinner at the Governor's Mansion on November 3, 1974.

The governor seemed a little defensive about his use of the highway patrol plane. D. C. Thomas asked him to comment on that. In a long, rambling answer sprinkled with references to General Motors and Xerox, Hall contended, "I felt that this was proper state business. I'm not going to ask a man who's going to put $20 million dollars into Oklahoma to come up here on a Greyhound Bus." (Hall conveniently ignored Mooney's testimony that the matter of Taylor's plan had never been mentioned yet.)

"Part way through the dinner," Hall said, "Mr. Taylor proceeded to outline in general terms a plan which he thought would benefit the state of Oklahoma."

Hall testified that when he left for Japan on November 7th, he had someone in his office arrange a conference between Max Stange and W. W. Taylor. He returned on November 19th and met with attorney Frank McDivitt to discuss what Randy Floyd had told Jo Hall about John Rogers being pressured to frame him. He said that on the 22nd of November Rogers called him about the Taylor proposal, and Hall told him he thought it was a good plan.

Fireworks went off when Burkett objected to Thomas's attempt to bring in some hearsay testimony. The issue was whether Hall could report the contents of a conversation with John Rogers that took place before Rogers began his undercover work, i.e., became a government agent. Burkett argued it was inappropriate.

"Let the record show," D. C. Thomas testily shot off, "I'm sure the United States Prosecutor would like for me to try this lawsuit the way he wants to try it, but I'm not going to try it that way. I'm going to try it the right way."

Judge Daugherty fired right back, "You're going to try it the way I tell you!"

Chastened, Thomas corrected himself, "I'm sorry, the way the Court tells me to try it."

When asked about the December 2nd Fort Worth trip, Hall said he went to see Taylor and Mooney for two reasons. One was to discuss Palo Mesa because Taylor had never seen the architectural plans, and the other was to discuss Taylor's investment proposal. Hall denied having a conversation with Rogers in the Blue Room on December 3, or any other place in which "I offered him money or he offered me money."

Hall described a number of "red flags" that caused him to be suspicious of Rogers. One was on December 10 when Rogers asked for his help refinancing a building he owned in Midwest City. Another occurred in California on December 18th or 19th in a telephone conversation--Hall couldn't remember who initiated it--in which they discussed the investment plan; he said this raised his suspicions because it was the first time in the four years Hall had been governor that Rogers had ever pushed a retirement plan.

Hall said that after he came back to Oklahoma and talked to Rogers by phone, Rogers said a peculiar thing, namely, that "8-1/4 percent would be better for us." "For the state of Oklahoma?" Hall said he asked, and Rogers said, "No, for us." Hall asserted, "This was the third red flag."

As might be expected, Hall put his own "spin" on the conversations about contacting the various board members. Always, he said, his primary interest was what was good for the state of Oklahoma. He denied he made any deals with Taylor to split the profits, denied a deal with Mooney, and denied any bribe conversation with Rogers.

On the 26th of December, Hall said, he was in Park City, Utah, on a family ski trip when Rogers called and mentioned Mooney and money in the same sentence. That was the fourth red flag, Hall said. "I was surprised but I was not surprised."

Thomas asked, "What do you mean by that?"

"I immediately knew that there was something wrong," Hall explained, "but I didn't know whether it was an extortion, a bribe, or an attempt to frame me--or all three."

On the 27th of December, Hall said he got a call from Gerry Strain, his secretary, asking him to call Bob Sanders, and she gave him a telephone number. When he called the number, he got Sanders at Jamil's Restaurant in Oklahoma City. They had a conversation about Rogers trying to frame him. He said that was the fifth red flag.

Q: "What did you do after talking to Bob Sanders?"

A: "I began to think over all that had happened in relation to this whole situation. So, I called Kevin Mooney in Fort Worth, Texas, and told him that Rogers was trying to frame me."

Q: "What did Mooney say?"

A: "He acted surprised."

Hall went on to say, "I determined that I would not alert the federal officers that I knew of their plan against me. And so from that point on, I tried to avoid any telephone conversation in which they might learn that I knew for certain that they were trying to frame me.''

Upon his return to Oklahoma City, according to Hall, he contacted attorney Frank McDivitt and told him to contact the Watergate Committee. Thomas asked why the Watergate Committee, and Hall stated, "I felt that the attorney general was a part of the frame. I felt that Mr. William Burkett was a part of the frame. I felt that the FBI, acting under his direction, would not give credence to my story."

When Hall was going through the capitol and saying goodbye to people on January 10th, he said that he encountered John Rogers in the hallway. "I told him that we had a surprise for Derryberry regarding the federal grand jury." However, Hall said he never told Rogers what that surprise would be. Later that day, Hall went to Dallas, and from there had another telephone conversation with Rogers. "He asked me if I still intended to file a lawsuit against Mr. Burkett and the federal government... and I told him that we did," Hall contended.

Hall testified that January 13, Inauguration Day, was a very sad but busy day. He was kept busy in his office greeting well-wishers and signing last-minute appointments, commissions, etc. Rogers came by and talked with him, and also called him later at the Mansion.

Q: "Did you, at any time, use your influence as governor, your position as governor of this state, to try to extort or influence a scheme for a bribe?"

A: "I did not at any time take any such action to that effect."

THOMAS: "Your Honor, I have no further questions."

"The Court will be in recess until two o'clock."

The lawyers quickly took their places after lunch, eager for the battle royale to begin. Burkett was already standing at the podium going over his notes when David Hall climbed blithely back onto the witness stand as if nothing unusual were happening. He seemed totally unconcerned that he was about to undergo a vigorous cross examination. Judge Daugherty reminded him that he was still under the same oath earlier administered.

Burkett began by asking him about his theory that he was the victim of some grand government conspiracy. Burkett did so because that theory characterized Hall's whole defense, and Burkett thought it so ludicrous that he wanted to expose it to the jury.

Q: "Mr. Hall, do I understand that you accuse the Department of Justice, the Federal Bureau of Investigation, me, the Attorney General of Oklahoma, and John Rogers of conspiring to frame you in this case?"

A: "That is correct, Mr. Burkett."

Burkett's style was aggressively mocking. He focused on the ridiculous character of his defense.

Q: "Do you contend that the Internal Revenue Service is a part of this conspiracy?"

A: "I do."

Q: "Do you contend that the Secret Service is a part of this conspiracy?"

A: "I do not. I have no evidence that they are."

Q: "Do you contend that the Customs Service is a part of this?"

A "I do not."

Q: "Do you contend that the Alcohol, Tobacco and Firearms Bureau is a part of this conspiracy?"

A: "I do not."

Q: "Do you contend that the Postal Inspector's Service is a part of the conspiracy?"

A: "There's a question about mail tampering in some instances."

Q: "Do you contend that the Drug Enforcement Administration is a part of this conspiracy?"

A: "I do not."

Q: "Do you contend that R. Kevin Mooney is a part of this conspiracy?"

A: "I think he became a part of it later on."

Q: "At what time did he become a part of it?"
A: "After he had entered his plea and you had talked to him."
The fact is that Kevin Mooney was not arrested until January 14 and did not enter his plea until January 21, but Hall made his initial appearance on the 17th for the purpose of fixing bail--four days prior to Mooney's plea. By deliberately confusing and blending two different time frames, Hall appeared to be providing himself with a basis to plant the idea of entrapment in the jury's minds.

Actually, the prosecution would have loved for Hall to claim that he was entrapped. The entrapment defense is a "Yes, but..." defense. It requires, as a first step, that you admit that you committed the crime, and then you say, "Yes, but I was entrapped." It is a very difficult defense, seldom used, and even more seldom successful.

Burkett asked Hall to describe what the so-called conspirators did to frame him in this case.

"I think that you offered immunity to John Rogers in return for him putting the frame on me. I think you brought pressure on Mr. Rogers so that he, in fact, would perjure himself."

"Is it your contention that I knowingly used his perjured testimony to prosecute you?"

"I'm not accusing you of perjury, Mr. Burkett. I think you were a willing dupe."

Hall said he thought his telephones were--and continue to be--bugged. Burkett asked whom he reported this to, and he said he asked Frank McDivitt to inform the Watergate special prosecutor--although he had no knowledge of whether or not this was done. When asked if D. C. Thomas had advised him that the above-named government agencies had searched their files and found no electronic surveillance of either him or Mr. Taylor, Hall acknowledged receiving that report but still insisted his phones were being tapped.

Using the gentle art of cross-examination, Burkett patiently coaxed out of Hall his version of the events beginning with the time of his initial conversation with Mooney and ending with his last conversation with John Rogers on January 13. Suffice it to say that he had a glib explanation for everything, and always foremost in his mind, or so he said, was what was good for the state of Oklahoma.

Sparks began to fly when Burkett started confronting Hall with the inconsistencies between his testimony on the stand and the incriminating words on the tape transcripts. For example, on December 18th Hall was contacting board members from his vacation spa in California and urging them to vote for the plan. In a recorded conversation, Rogers asked him if he was going to call Leo Winters. Hall said, "No, that would raise a white flag to Leo and he would go to Larry Derryberry."

Q: "Why would you say that? What were you referring to?"

A: "I felt Derryberry was a political enemy, as well as a part of this conspiracy."

Q: "Do you feel that Leo Winters was a political enemy?"

A: "Absolutely not."

Q: "Then why would Mr. Winters go to Larry Derryberry if you called him about this?"

A: "I had an apprehension about asking Mr. Winters to do anything at that point."

Q: "What was your apprehension, sir?"

A: "Well, I had no control over him."

Q: "And you thought that if you told Leo Winters about this that he would go and tell Larry Derryberry, and Larry Derryberry would know what this scheme was?"

A: "No. No."

Despite extensive questioning along this line, Hall was never able to come up with a satisfactory explanation of what he meant when he said he was afraid Winters would go to the attorney general. Obviously, from the prosecution's standpoint, Burkett wanted the jury to infer that Hall had something to hide.

The next verbal clash took place over the subtle difference between "influence" and "advocacy." Hall denied he was trying to exercise influence over the vote of the board members by making those calls to them, yet he affirmed, "You know, I'm an advocate of the pension and I advocated that pension."

"An advocate is someone who is attempting to persuade, is it not?" Burkett retorted. He raised that issue because in the tape of December 18 Hall told John Rogers if he had a "hammer on them" he would have used it. But in his direct testimony, he denied he ever used that term with Rogers.

Q: "Governor, as a matter of fact, didn't you tell Mr. Rogers that the trouble with getting the board members to vote for this was that you were going out of office?"

A: "That's true."

Q: "Didn't you tell him if you were still in office, you wouldn't cajole a J. O. Spiller, that you wouldn't cajole a Jim Cook, that you wouldn't cajole other board members, didn't you tell Mr. Rogers that you would just call them on the phone and say, 'Okay, buster, you vote that mother, I don't care what they say, or you won't be here next week?'"

A: "In the case of Mr. Spiller, that is correct."

In his direct testimony, Hall had insisted that Rogers was the one moving things along, and that he, Hall, was merely playing along in order to lead Rogers into a trap. So Burkett called his attention to a conversation that took place on December 19th. "Hall: 'I've got one down and two to go. I don't want you to call a meeting but I'm right in the process of calling them. I think I will have them called in the next 15 minutes.'"

Burkett asked him if that was correct. Hall insisted he wanted to see a transcript, and the judge ordered his attorney to provide him with a copy. (Again, the prosecution derived a measure of personal satisfaction from the fact that although Judge Daugherty had not allowed the jury to have copies, the transcripts were freely and officially used by the court--which, in effect, was a tacit endorsement.)

Q: "You testified that it seemed unusual to you that Rogers was so interested in this proposal, is that correct?"

A: "That is correct."

Q: "Now, he was chairman of the board that was going to consider this proposal, was he not?"

A: "That is correct."

Q: "You, on the other hand, had no vote in it, did you not?"

A: "I had no vote, but I had a tremendous interest in it."

Q: "I see. Tremendous interest. What was the source of this tremendous interest?"

A: "I was Governor of the state. I should do everything in my power to make that board operate efficiently and make money."

Q: "Had you ever talked to any of the board members about their investments, about the matters that they were considering, investments that they were considering prior to this time?"

A: "No. On that board I never had knowledge, except on this one, of such an investment."

Q: "Did you ever make an inquiry about the investments that they were making?"

A: "No. That's the only one."

The point Burkett was trying to get across to the jury was that it was perfectly normal for the chairman of the board--in this case, John Rogers--to be concerned about the investments; what was abnormal was the interest of the Governor in this particular investment, inasmuch as this was the first time in four years--and only a few days before leaving office--that Hall insinuated himself into the board's decision process, and he used extraordinary means to do so.

After the afternoon recess, D. C. Thomas squabbled with Burkett over the prosecution's plan to play back something Hall said on one of the tapes. In a sidebar conference, Thomas objected that it had already been played to the jury. Judge Daugherty asked Burkett, "Do you think you are entitled to go over this evidence more than once? Wouldn't it be repetitious?" "No, sir," the prosecutor replied. "If this were a document or a piece of tangible evidence, nobody would suggest that I couldn't hand it to the witness and ask him to explain it or comment on it."

That was one argument Burkett lost. "It's the same effect as live testimony," the judge ruled. "I don't believe I should permit you to do this." The adverse ruling did not pose a major setback for Burkett, however, because he still had access to the transcripts, and so far no one had disputed their accuracy.

It seemed that Hall's interest in pushing the Taylor proposal involved more than just the $31,250 he stood to collect as a finder's fee. By his own testimony, there was an implied *quid pro quo*--you help me and I'll help you--kind of arrangement. That is to say, if Hall could get Taylor's plan through OPERS, Taylor would help him get financing for his project at Palo Mesa in California. So when the trial routine resumed, Burkett asked Hall about Palo Mesa. "What would have been the profit to you personally?"

Hall said his profit would be somewhere in the neighborhood of $700,000.

The ludicrous character and hollowness of Hall's "conspiracy-to-frame-me" defense was once again exposed to the jury by a series of questions about whom he contacted in reference to the supposed frame-up. The questions were intended to show that Hall's claim was a mere pretense, and that any rational citizen who wasn't trying to cover up something would have reported the situation to someone in authority. Moreover, Hall, as Governor, had direct access to any number of officials to whom he could have complained.

Q: "Do you contend that the Director of Public Safety is a part of this conspiracy against you?"

A: "No, I do not."

Q: "Do you contend that the Oklahoma State Bureau of Investigation was a part of the conspiracy?"

A: "A portion of that bureau."

Q: "What portion of the bureau?"

A: "Agent Tom Puckett, the executive officer of the Crime Bureau."

Q: So, you didn't talk to any law enforcement agency in the

state of Oklahoma?''

A: "That is correct."

Q: "Did you talk to Mr. Curtis Harris[2] about it?"

A: "No, I did not."

Q: "You know Mr. Harris, do you not?"

A: "I know him very well."

Q: "Did you discuss it with Justice Simms of the Supreme Court?"

A: "I did not."

Q: "Or E. Melvin Porter of the State Senate?"

A: "I did not."

Q: "Or any reputable, prominent person in the state of Oklahoma?"

A: "Frank McDivitt."

Q: "Is Mr. McDivitt a law enforcement officer?"

A: "No, he is not."

Burkett went back over the conversation between Hall and Rogers on December 19th, the one in which he said, "I don't want you to call a meeting but I'm in the process of calling them." The line of questioning was intended to show that Hall was the person who was firmly in command and really running the show. A copy of the transcript was placed in front of him.

Q: "Now at the bottom of the third page, did Mr. Rogers say, 'But J. O. Spiller was really the bad guy. I mean, he doesn't think it's a bad deal but his remarks were that in the waning days of an administration, we're not going to invest in all this stuff.' Did he say that?"

A: "Yes."

Q: "Referring to page four, sir. You made a comment to that, did you not, Governor?"

A: "I said, 'Well, that sorry bastard.'"

Q: "Did Mr. Rogers then say, 'Cook just told you he was going to, and then he just took the easy way out and didn't show?'"

A: "I don't recall that particular line."

Q: "Do you recall then you said, 'Well, that dirty bastard?'"

A: "Yes, I said that."

Q: "Why the comment?"

A: "I don't know why I said that."

That last answer was Hall's constant refrain throughout the cross-examination--"I don't know why I said that." The simple fact of the matter was that he was caught with his hand in the cookie jar, and there simply wasn't any explanation for it. So, about the only excuse he could possibly give was, "I don't know why I said that."

The pattern of questioning in cross-examination moves always in narrowing circles, ever more tightly focused. The object is to mine the truth, not undermine it. Accordingly, Burkett revisited for a third time the issue of whom did Hall talk to about his supposed frame-up, and when did he talk to them.

Q: "Was there a member of your staff with whom you had a particular confidence and with whom you discussed political strategy?"

A: "Oh, there were several members."

Q: "Who were they, sir?"

A: "Of the immediate staff, Dan Rambo, Ed Hardy to some extent, Geraldine Strain, my administrative assistant. I would say those three, basically, of the senior staff; although I have discussed political strategy with Bob Sculley. I discussed it with Betty Ward. I discussed it with Bill Crain. I discussed it with any number of people."

Q: "Did you discuss with any of these people Mr. Taylor's proposal?"

A: "No, I did not."

Hall doggedly clung to his thesis that he was the innocent victim of a conspiracy to frame him, a conspiracy led by John Rogers. It was important, therefore, for the prosecution to demonstrate to the jury that he was in this thing up to his ears--that it was Hall, not Rogers, who was directing the scheme. One way to do this was to produce evidence that Hall was

directing--or attempting to direct--actions which would cause the
officers at First National Bank to give their approval to the
investment plan, which was the only thing holding up the deal
from going through. Again, the government had the tapes.

Q: "Did you have this conversation with Mr. Rogers on the
evening of the 23rd, you said, 'Now I'll tell you what we'll do if
they don't approve it.' Rogers: 'Okay.' Hall: "We'll just get five
votes and we'll change that [account] back down to Liberty Bank.
I can do that.' Did you tell him that?''

A: "I told him that."

Q: "Why did you tell him that, Governor?''

A: "I thought that if First National Bank selfishly would not
approve a plan good for Oklahoma, the account ought to be put
with another bank."

Q: "Now, then, did you say further, 'You can change it to the
Liberty Bank and Liberty can tell you it's a good investment.' Did
you say something to that effect?''

A: "Yes, I did."

Q: "Then did you say this, Governor: 'And... if they're going
to be a horse's ass about it, you know, for that matter, you could
dump the account and wait a month or two to do the thing with
them'?''

A: "I recall those words."

Q: "Well, did you go on to say that 'because if they won't help
us, I would just as soon punish them'?''

A: "I believe I said that."

Further questioning along this line elicited the admission that
Hall also talked about getting Leo Winters involved because "this
is something he can do to help us that doesn't show on the
surface." When Burkett asked him what he meant by that
reference to not showing on the "surface," Hall tried lamely to
brush it off as, "I was mad at First National, that's why I said
that."

Finally, Burkett asked him, "Who's in charge here, Governor,
you or John Rogers?'' "John Rogers,'' he insisted.

"But he's asking you what to do, and you're telling him, is he not?"

"Yes, sir."

"If you're at a stopping point, we should recess for the evening," the judge decreed. Wearing his most solemn judicial expression he gave his usual instructions to the jury--"You're under instructions not to discuss the case among yourselves until it's submitted to you, nor with anyone not a member of the jury at any time while you are sitting on the case as a juror. This includes your families and anyone else.... Also, you're to keep your minds free and open and do not form any opinion in the case one way or another until you have heard all the evidence and the case is submitted to you."

To the attorneys and assembled visitors, the judge said, "Everyone in the courtroom will please remain seated until the jury is retired."

Jim Peters leaned over to Burkett, "Watch the jury when they go by Hall."

The jury exited the courtroom through a door at the north end, which required them to file right past the witness stand with Hall still on it. Peters whispered, "See, they're not looking at him, they're not making eye contact." Sure enough, they weren't. To a trained observer, that was a strong indication that the members of the jury were not buying Hall's story.

   ...Friday, February 7, 1975.
   The Courtroom.   Hall, back in the witness box for the second day, wore a different suit and a different demeanor. Gone was the air of confidence and self-assurance. Now he appeared scared.

It was characteristic of David Hall to make up the truth as he went along, and at times he could be very convincing. After all, he wouldn't have climbed as far up the political ladder as he had--even mentioned as a possible vice presidential candidate--if he weren't able to inspire confidence in people. Therefore, it was necessary for the prosecution to undermine his veracity.

Nowhere was his convincing posture more evident than when,

during direct testimony, he described an idyllic family scene surrounding his telephone conversation with John Rogers on December 26th, the day after Christmas. He was in a condominium in Park City, Utah. Prompted by his attorney, D. C. Thomas, Hall had averred, "I was standing in the kitchen of the condominium, between the stove portion and the sink portion, right at that point, holding the phone up."

"Was Jo there, your wife?" Thomas had asked.

"Yes, she was."

"Kids there?"

"Yes, sir."

"I mean physically right there?"

"Yes. They were all there, they were all right there around the phone."

How could one possibly doubt his memory of that vivid a scene? So, Burkett got him to repeat that story for the jury. He even elaborated on it: "We were all dressed and ready to go out to the ski lifts in our ski clothes, in the kitchen putting on our gloves when the phone rang and a call came in from John Rogers."

"The call to Mr. Rogers' office on the 26th was about 13 minutes long, was it not?

"If the toll reflects that, I'm sure it's accurate."

As a former prosecutor himself, David Hall should have been smart enough to sense Burkett was about to spring a trap on him. "But you're sure, you remember being in the kitchen and the family there in their ski clothes ready to go to the slopes, you remember that very well?"

"I sure do, because they were very anxious for me to get off the phone."

That's when Burkett exposed his lie. "Governor, would you look at Exhibit 44, please. Why is it that the telephone toll records show that telephone call was not made from Park City, Utah, but Salt Lake City, Utah, that day?"

"On the 26th?"

"Yes, sir," Burkett replied. "The fact is, Governor, you made that call from the motel in Salt Lake City, did you not?"

Whether Hall was in Salt Lake City or Park City on that day really didn't make any difference as far as the content of the conversation was concerned; what was important was that Hall was shown to be an ingenious fabricator of the truth. A seed of doubt was planted in the jury's minds, and from now on, Burkett hoped, they would be increasingly skeptical of anything he might say.

Hall looked as if his handsome face had begun to melt.

The prosecution got into the substance of that December 26th conversation from Utah. The conversation began with Rogers saying, "I told the bank I would move the account. Any luck with Leo?"

Hall replied, "Yeah, Leo is going to go with us. Try to have a meeting before the first of the year."

"No meeting is necessary, we've already approved it," Rogers said.

"Well then I think you ought to go ahead and execute what needs to be done just as quickly as you can."

"I think that Mooney ought to get the money from Taylor."

Hall quickly cut him off, "Okay, just don't talk about that."

When Burkett asked Hall what he meant by that, his explanation was a bit far-reaching. He avowed that when he heard Rogers mention Mooney and money in the same sentence, he decided that there was a frame going on, and thereafter he was merely trying to keep Rogers talking so he could get Rogers to say something that would prove that it was a frame. In a nutshell, Hall was now trying to portray himself in the role of an investigator conducting an undercover investigation of a crime, rather than as a conspirator participating in a crime. In wrestling this move would be called a "reversal."

The problem with that explanation was that it didn't fit the facts--in particular his admonition, "Don't talk about that." If Hall were truly trying to prove a frame, he would have drawn Rogers out about the case rather than try to shut him up.

To show up the ridiculousness of Hall's claim, Burkett asked him a series of rapid-fire questions that any sensible, law-abiding lawyer would have asked if offered a bribe:

"Did you ask him 'What money'?"

"No, I did not."

"Did you say, 'What in the world are you talking about'?"

"No, I did not."

"Did you say, 'Are you out of your mind'?"

"No, I did not."

"Did you say, 'Are you trying to make a bribe'?"

"No."

"Did you say, 'Are you extorting money from someone'?"

"No, I did not."

"Did you say, 'Are you trying to frame me for something'?"

"No."

"You didn't even break off your connection with him, did you, Mr. Hall?" (That was more of a statement than a question.)

"No."

Now that he had crowned himself with the white hat of an independent prosecutor, so to speak, David Hall clung doggedly to this new tack. To every question about why he made this or that incriminating statement, Hall invariably answered, "I was leading John Rogers on."

For example, when Rogers said in the December 26th conversation, "I'm worried about this," Hall assured him, "Don't worry, people that don't play fair and keep their word get in trouble." Hall's glib explanation was that what he had suspected he had now decided was true, and he was trying to prolong the activity as long as he could to check it out. "If I had mentioned to Rogers that I knew what he was talking about," he said, "then I would have no chance of proving it."

"So from that point on, its all just scenario?" Burkett asked.

"From here on, it is," he replied.

A little later in the cross examination, Hall was asked, "Didn't you testify on direct examination that you wrote this note ["We

are bugged''] because if those conspiring against you knew that
you knew, you would be unable to get evidence to present to Mr.
Ruth, the [Watergate] special prosecutor?''

Hall solemnly asserted, ''Mr. Burkett, I felt. that if you were
tipped off that you were trying to be a part of the frame and a
willing dupe, that Rogers might not give enough information so
that later on I would be unable to prove to the [Watergate]
committee what happened.''

Following the morning recess, Burkett returned to explore in
greater detail this novel theme that Hall was now putting forward
about conducting his own private investigation. He asked about
the conversation of January 9th.

''Rogers said, 'But I don't know that they won't screw you,'
and you replied, 'Yeah that's true. Yeah, that's true.' Are you still
leading him?''

''Yeah, just leading him on.''

Next, he took Hall to the January 10th conversation with
Rogers. ''Then did you say, 'Everything is going to be all right.
That's what I understand. We confirmed. We confirmed.' What
were you telling him?''

''I was just leading him on, leading him on.''

''And you said, 'But I think everything is in good shape.' Still
leading him on?''

''Absolutely.''

''Did you say, 'That is as certain as the sun comes up in the
east'?''

''I hoped that I was misleading him.''

Burkett turned next to several incriminating statements in the
conversation that took place on the evening of January 10 while
Hall was in Dallas. Rogers started to talk about the ''rinky-dink''
way Mooney and Taylor had proposed paying him off. Hall
interjected, ''Listen, don't talk to me on the phone about
anything.''

Q: ''This was so Rogers wouldn't know you were onto the
deal, is that right?''

A: ''Yes, that is correct.''

Q: "You didn't want him to know you were onto it so you told him not to talk about it."

A: "If all of a sudden I changed and wanted to discuss it with him on the phone, Mr. Burkett, he would have known something was up."

Q: "Did you say, 'I don't know what they told you or what they haven't said to you, but what I said to you in our last two conversations is what you can rely on. I wouldn't pay any attention to what they're saying'?"

A: "That is correct. I was leading him on."

Q: "What did you mean by that?"

A: "I wanted Rogers to have trust in me so that this would continue on. One of the problems I was concerned with was that he would abort this before we had the information on him."

Another damaging exchange occurred in the January 10th conversation. Although it didn't go to the heart of the conspiracy charge, it did serve to reveal Hall's venality, and it further undermined his credibility in the eyes of the jury.

In this conversation, John Rogers had been talking about his father, John M. Rogers, State Auditor and Inspector, who was the subject of a lawsuit that might force him out of office. Hall told Rogers, "First thing I would get your dad to do, if that lawsuit doesn't stop, is audit [Governor-elect] Boren's account when he was representative."

"Did you say that?" Burkett asked.

"Yes, I said that."

"Why did you suggest to him he audit Boren's account?"

"I was just leading him on throughout this whole conversation...."

"Now, Rogers said, 'Can you do that?' and you said, 'Sure. Check his telephone calls to see if any of them are personal, check his travel claims to see if he's high, and I'll bet you a dollar he did what everybody does, signed his travel claims in blank'."

"That's right, I remember I said that."

Burkett surmised that the jury would be repulsed by the

outlandish idea of Hall ordering an audit of the incoming governor's financial records. It was an act of pure pettiness that didn't have reference to anything.

The cross examination was wending its way towards a close. David Hall had not been a very credible witness. But how could he be? Those tapes were heavy, heavy evidence, and he wasn't able to offer any coherent explanations for the terrible things he said.

In the final exchange, Burkett focused on Kevin Mooney's role in the supposed conspiracy against Hall. "You testified, Mr. Hall, that you believed that Kevin Mooney became a part of the conspiracy against you after he entered a plea of guilty in this court?"

"That's correct, Mr. Burkett."

"What do you believe he did to further the conspiracy?"

"I believe he testified falsely."

"Do you contend that Mr. Mooney pled guilty to an offense of which he was not guilty?"

"I don't know that in fact. I didn't advise him."

"Is it your contention, and you are telling this jury, that you believe Mr. Mooney pled guilty to a felony in this court, subjecting himself to all of the consequences, perhaps the least of which is disbarment, as a part of a plot to cause you to be prosecuted and convicted?"

"That is not my contention."

"Do you know Rooney McInereny?" Burkett asked.

"I know him well," Hall replied.

"Former justice of the Supreme Court of Oklahoma?"

"Yes."

"Are you telling this court that after Mr. McInereny had his client enter a plea of guilty, that he then allowed him to perjure himself?"

"I don't think he did it intentionally."

"Oh, another willing dupe, Governor?"

"Absolutely, Mr. Burkett."

"Rooney McInereny, Justice Rooney McInereny, a willing dupe?"

"No. I think...."

"Who is the willing dupe?"

"You are!"

That started another prickly exchange in which Jimmy Linn--even though he was not Hall's attorney--voiced a complaint, "Judge, they are arguing." Judge Daugherty was imperturbable. "The witness is not giving direct answers, that brings about the argument," he said. Turning towards Hall, he admonished, "If you will answer the question, we will get along a lot better."

Burkett resumed his questioning. "Now, Mr. Hall, if Mooney didn't join this conspiracy until after he pled guilty, how do you explain his statements about your participation in this payoff scheme made to Rogers and discussed with Mr. Rogers and Mr. Taylor on the tapes which we have heard--all made before he knew he would be arrested?"

"I think that Mr. Rogers planted that story on him early in the relationship between Mr. Mooney and Mr. Taylor."

"Have you heard any conversations on tape recordings here in which Mr. Rogers planted some story on Kevin Mooney?"

"No, I have not."

Hall looked beaten.

"No further questions, Your Honor," Burkett told the court. As he slid into his seat, Jim Peters leaned over and whispered, "It's like being on the *Titanic*, but without the band."

There was virtually no redirect or recross-examination by either side. After a few desultory questions, D. C. Thomas announced, "Your Honor, our defendant rests."

The judge intoned, "Defendant Hall rests, Ladies and Gentlemen of the jury, which means you have heard the evidence presented to you on behalf of Defendant Hall."

For David Hall, that meant the long, humiliating ordeal was over.

§ § §

12

The Defense - Taylor

...Friday, March 7, 1975

The Courtroom. The jury had just returned from lunch; some of the jurors appeared to be drowsy. Now came W. W. Taylor's defense. Everybody wondered what kind of defense Jimmy Linn would put on for his client.

The judge instructed Linn to call his first witness in behalf of Defendant Taylor. Momentary confusion prevailed as Linn had to step out into the hallway to find Dick Finlay. Finlay was nowhere to be found. Linn apologized, "I could not find Mr. Finlay, Your Honor. We call Mr. Rex Scott."

Rex Scott, 35, identified himself as a mortgage broker who worked with Doc Taylor's company in Dallas. He was paid on a commission-only basis. Scott testified that he had a conversation with Taylor on or about the first of December. Linn asked, "What did he tell you about that?"

Hardly had Linn gotten this question out of his mouth before Bill Burkett bounced to his feet, objecting that Scott's answer would call for hearsay evidence. All the lawyers gathered at the bench while Linn and Burkett wrangled it out before the judge, outside the hearing of the jury. After listening to the arguments, Judge Daugherty decided he would allow the testimony--but only to the extent it went to Taylor's motive and not to the truth of the fact.

When the lawyers resumed their places but before questioning could begin again, the judge made a little speech to the jury:

Ladies and Gentlemen of the jury, what Defendant Taylor

would have told this witness on November 8th would
ordinarily be hearsay testimony except that the Court is
allowing it to come in for the sole and only purpose of the
jury determining the intent and motive of Defendant Taylor,
as shown by these remarks at that time, and it is not presented
to establish the truth of the statements made, merely to
demonstrate his state of mind, his intent and motive as of the
date that the statements were made.

What did that really mean? Burkett felt that the point was hard
to grasp and hold, as mercurial as David Hall's silvery hair.

After all of that hullabaloo, Scott's testimony was rather
innocuous. He said that Taylor told him about an earlier meeting
in which the Secretary of State indicated to Taylor that he held a
job that did not pay enough to support his family, and that he had
to get some money from somewhere else.

The future pattern of Jimmy Linn's defense strategy was
beginning to unfold. He was going to contend that (1) Taylor had
a good plan, and (2) Taylor was a lamb that fell among the
wolves.

Accordingly, through his lead-off witnesses, he wanted to plant
in the jury's minds the idea that Rogers had his hand out even
before the conspiracy began on December 2nd.

Burkett had doubts about how this kind of testimony was going
to help Linn's client. Even if Linn were able to convince the jury
that Taylor's state of mind was that Rogers had his hand out, the
facts would then show that Taylor walked into the deal with his
eyes wide open, and hence he was far from being the innocent
victim that Linn would have them believe him to be.

Jim Peters moved in to conduct the cross examination of Scott.
Peters was low-key, thorough, very precise, and tended to dissect
a witness with the skill of a top surgeon. Peters patiently coaxed
from Scott the admission that Taylor paid him a one-percent
commission on all monies he brought in--which was precisely the
same percentage as Taylor agreed to pay David Hall for bringing

in $10 million of the state's money.

Linn's next two witnesses were both employees of Taylor's firm in Dallas; they, too, were paid on the same one-percent commission basis.

Richard Finlay made his appearance. He said he had accompanied Taylor to Oklahoma City for his meetings with Max Stange and John Rogers on November 8th. He testified that the meeting was very brief, and at the conclusion Rogers remarked, "You realize, gentlemen, that the earnings I make as a public official do not begin to meet the expenses that I have for a living." He said that when he and Taylor left, they mutually concluded that this "sounded like a man who had his hand out for some money."

Finlay acknowledged that no specific amount of money was mentioned, and that they left an offering circular with Rogers. He admitted that he never suggested the matter be reported to law-enforcement officials.

William Boone didn't add much to what had been said before. He testified that on December 23 and again on January 3, Taylor told him that the project was progressing satisfactorily but that "one state official wanted a cash payment for the commitment." He said he asked Taylor what he was going to do about it, and Taylor said he didn't like it but there wasn't much he could do.

Burkett did the cross-examination of Boone. He reported that Taylor named John Rogers as being the state official who was seeking a payoff, but he admitted that Taylor never told him about the $31,250 check that had been written to Mooney.

Three character witness were paraded before the jury: James Augar, a Dallas architect; John Palmer, a Dallas real estate and investment broker; and Robert W. Easley of Oline, New York, a special labor assistant for the NAACP. Their testimony was a foregone conclusion; namely, that W. W. Taylor was a fine, upstanding individual with a good reputation in the community.

The jury listened courteously but did not appear to be impressed.

It began to appear as if Taylor's witnesses all came in sets of three. Maybe Jimmy Linn thought there was something magical about the number three. First, there were the three employees--Scott, Finlay and Boone; then three character witnesses, Augar, Palmer and Easley; and now another three persons were lined up to testify that Taylor's investment plan was a good plan.

Linn announced David McClain as his next witness. Duly sworn, McClain stated that he was an attorney with the Dallas-based firm of Wynn and Jaffee, and that his firm had prepared the documents for the Oklahoma project. He told the court he was familiar with the plan, and the only way the fund could lose money on its investment would be if the U.S. government failed to perform on its guarantee.

Cross-examination was relatively brief. The prosecution's position was that it didn't matter whether or not Taylor's plan was a good plan--its quality was irrelevant. What *was* important for the prosecutors was to show that a conspiracy to commit a crime had taken place using this vehicle, that Hall and Taylor did willfully, knowingly, and intentionally conspire to commit a felony, regardless of the quality of the outcome. Accordingly, there was no point to their making a big deal out of the plan or being led down the "primrose path" of arguing its merits; rather, they were willing only to argue as to what the conspirators did to further that plan.

George Hibbard, Executive Vice President of the First National Bank of Pekin, Illinois, was the next witness. He testified that he was familiar with the plan, that his bank was to be the custodial trustee, and that the investment would be entirely safe. No cross-examination.

Then came a lawyer from Arlington, Virginia, Sara Knight, former assistant general counsel to the Small Business Administration (SBA). She testified that not only was she familiar with the plan that Taylor had submitted to Oklahoma, but she had actually helped to draft the regulations that governed the plan while she worked for the SBA. She went into great detail about the purpose of the small business programs to get people off welfare, and that after leaving her job at the SBA she worked with Taylor on several projects around the country.

Under cross-examination, Burkett got her to admit that the plan was complicated. He asked her if it would be readily understood by someone not familiar with it on the basis of a more or less cursory examination. She conceded that it was not easily understandable by the ordinary laymen, or even the average lawyer. Burkett was, of course, leading to the fact that Hall never spent enough time examining the details of this plan to be able to actually evaluate it, yet he was recommending it and going to extraordinary efforts to achieve its adoption.

Also, he got her to concede that if somebody defaulted on a mortgage, although the plan itself wouldn't lose any money, the U.S. government would have to cough up the money--and, she said, the government "gets its money from you and me and all the other millions of taxpayers." That last admission really didn't have any relevancy for the case at hand, but at least it took some edge off the defense's claim that this was a fool-proof plan. That business about the taxpayer losing money didn't set well with the jury.

"This might be a good time to take a recess," said Judge Daugherty. "It is now 3:40 p.m. Please be back in your seats at a quarter of four."

The honored jurors filed in, each to his or her own personal chair. W. W. Taylor stepped into the dock and was duly sworn. Plump, round-faced, smallish, fiftyish, polished forehead, balding hair slicked back, rimless eyeglasses, and wearing expensively tailored clothes, Taylor turned to flash a cherubic smile at the jury. The nickname "Doc," which had been with him since high school days, fit him like a glove.

Jimmy Linn led him through his family, educational, and work backgrounds, and then asked him to describe to the jury the investment plan that he proposed to the state of Oklahoma. Taylor went into great detail about how the plan was guaranteed by the U.S. government and that the state of Oklahoma could not possibly lose money on it.

Linn's client was well-rehearsed. With only minimal prodding by his attorney, Taylor recounted at length and in great detail his own version of the events leading up to his arrest. There really wasn't much to his testimony that the jury hadn't heard before; it's just that he remembered things differently from what previous witnesses had said.

For example, whereas Hall told the jury that he flew Taylor and Mooney up for dinner at the Mansion on November 3 expressly for the purpose of talking about Taylor's investment plan, as Taylor remembered it, it wasn't that way at all. "I eventually got to say something about *my* program," he said, "and I told him I was interested in meeting with the employees' retirement system." Apparently, that was the first mention of it to Hall.

As might be expected, Taylor denied ever discussing a $100,000 finder's fee with Mooney. He said that $100,000 would have been way out of line, that the most Mooney could expect to receive was $25,000--and that only if Mooney did all the paperwork.

Linn's next question seemed designed to get Taylor to say that every time he and Rogers got together, Rogers demanded money from him. "Yes, as we walked in [on November 8], we introduced ourselves and told him who we were, and he said 'You know, I'm a public official. When I first came into office I put all of my business interests in trust and it costs me twice as much to live as I make'." Taylor thought that was a prelude to asking for money.

O. B. Johnston scribbled a note to Burkett. *So what if they say Rogers was a crook, all that proves is that Taylor was a crook too. So who's the bigger crook, the guy who asks or the guy who pays?*

Taylor remembered that in the meeting of December 4, John Rogers again brought up the matter of his personal finances and told him, "If you help me, I help you." He said he immediately changed the topic because "I was there to sell my program, not to solve his problem."

Surprisingly, as precise and detailed as Taylor had been on the previous conversations, his memory suddenly failed him when it came to the meeting of December 18. Somehow, he kept thinking the meeting took place on the 20th. Jimmy Linn tried to refresh his memory, but Taylor still appeared befuddled.

Of course, having listened to the tape of that conversation, Burkett could readily understand why his mind didn't *want* to remember--that was the self-incriminating tape in which Taylor agreed to pay Rogers an extra $12,500 if he could get the deal through at eight percent.

"This is a good stopping point," Judge Daugherty interjected. "We will recess until Monday morning at 9:30."

...Monday, March 10, 1975

The Courtroom.   A blustery winter storm had blown in overnight, unleashing hail, snow and strong winds. "Good morning, Ladies and Gentlemen, I hope you all had a pleasant weekend," the judge intoned with a practiced voice. "Let the record show the jury is in the box, government present by counsel, both defendants present in person and by counsel."

With the court's permission, Jimmy Linn put on another character witness out of turn, a Dallas building contractor named George Jones who attended the same church as Taylor. He testified that Taylor was a peaceful and law-abiding citizen of good reputation. Then Taylor resumed the stand again.

Having had a weekend to think about it, Taylor pieced together a version of the story that he hoped would stand up. He knew, of course, that the jury had already heard the tape and that he would have to somehow explain away his own incriminating statements. So, he told the jury that when Rogers said the governor was going to split $50,000 with him, "I was surprised that he came out directly and said that. This was the first time I had ever heard anything about any $25,000 going to Rogers or $50,000 going to anybody. So, I tried to divert him from this conversation and started talking about rates and yields." When Rogers persisted, according to Taylor, "I said, 'I cannot pay you anything as a direct result of this placement because then I have to show it in the prospectus'." Taylor volunteered that this was a feeble attempt to fend him off. He said nothing about the additional $12,500, and Jimmy Linn didn't ask him.

Again on the 23rd of December, Taylor said, following the board's approval of the investment plan, Rogers made some more demands for payment. "I fenced around with him, and left to catch an airplane," he averred.

Linn gave Taylor an opportunity to challenge the most damning piece of evidence against his client. On December 30, Taylor was in Dallas attending a meeting at the First National Bank when a Mr. Wilson, one of the bank officers, opened the door and said, "There's a Mr. John Rogers from Oklahoma City on the telephone insisting on talking to you." Taylor excused himself, and took the call. Rogers told him, "I've got the bank's approval. The deal is done. Bring $31,250 and you can pick up the letter."

"This really shook me up," Taylor said, "because I was standing at another bank officer's desk, using his phone, and here was this man demanding money. So I decided that I couldn't divert Rogers or talk about something else, so I made him tell me the whole story so that I could report his activities to the highest authority I knew in Oklahoma, which was Governor Hall."

On that same day Taylor had his secretary draw a check for $31,250 to Kevin Mooney. "I knew I was going to have to do something to make Rogers believe that I might pay him if he would turn loose of that letter. So I went back to my office and had my secretary, Diane Gay, type a check to Kevin Mooney for $31,250. I did not sign the check. I folded up the check and put it in my billfold."

If the jury found this hard to believe, they gave no sign. They sat calmly listening to these carefully choreographed reminiscences of a man who said he never intended to pay any money, yet wrote a $31,250 check because there was a possibility that the whole program might blow up if he couldn't string Rogers along; a man who sent Mooney up to Oklahoma City on January 3rd to pick up the letter, and when Rogers wouldn't give it to him without the money, told Mooney to "forget the whole program and come home;" a man who six days later showed Mooney the $31,250 check and sent him back to Oklahoma City to pick up the trust agreements.

With little prodding from Linn, Taylor told a tearful tale of his humiliating arrest and arraignment in Jackson, Mississippi. "At 12:30 we walked out of the lunch room into the lobby [of the Downtowner Motel], and my associate and my attorney and I were standing there by the registration desk. My attorney left to get some documents, and these three or four fellows--I don't know how many there were--rushed up to me and grabbed me and asked if I was W. W. Taylor, and I said yes. They said, 'We're with the FBI,' and flashed a card, and grabbed me and took me out to the car. My associate ran up to the attorney, because he didn't hear them say they were FBI, and told him I had been kidnapped.

"The first thing they did was take me into this room where there was a whole bunch of people. They said they were with the United Press, the Associated Press, the television station, all of this sort of thing. My attorney asked, 'How did you know this man was going to be arrested?' They said, 'We got notification from our Oklahoma City office that the U.S. Attorney or someone in Oklahoma City had notified them and they wanted a lot of publicity on this arrest.'

"Finally, they took me to another room and we got with the magistrate. He started to fill out a form for a bond when someone stuck their head in the door and said, 'You're wanted on the phone'--not me, but the magistrate. He came back and said there was a phone call from the U.S. Attorney's office in Oklahoma City and they are insisting that your bond be set at $25,000 cash and no less."

Linn asked, "Did they get the publicity they wanted down there?"

"Yeah. I made the front page."

"...with the chains on," added Taylor, choking. He asked for a glass of water.

Perceiving that the witness was not in condition to go on, Judge Daugherty mercifully announced, "It's time for our morning recess; we will recess at this time."

After the break, Taylor recounted another poignant vignette designed to wring sympathy from the jury: "January 14th was my wife's birthday, and when they finally got the $25,000 bail up, I went out to the airport to catch a plane, and I was going into the gift shop to get my wife a little gift, and at the newsstand out in front of the gift shop there I was on the front page, full of pictures, belly chains, handcuffs, and all."

Linn was moving towards a conclusion. "Now, Mr. Taylor, have you ever been arrested before in your lifetime?"

"No, sir."

"Have you ever broken the law, to your knowledge, other than your one speeding ticket?"

"No, sir. Never have."

"Did you ever have any intent to corruptly bribe John Rogers or Governor Hall?"

"I never intended to corruptly bribe anybody, and I never intended to pay anybody."

"Do you have any conscience about anything that you think you've done wrong in this regard?"

"The only thing that I did wrong, which was morally wrong, was to lie to John Rogers when I told him I would help him with his building and things, because I never intended to."

"That is all," said Linn.

Bill Burkett rose to begin the government's cross-examination. His tone was crisply courteous. "Mr. Taylor, when did you form the corporation known as Guaranteed Investors Corporation?" Taylor said he formed it in August or October of 1974, he couldn't remember for sure.

"What are the assets of Guaranteed Investors Corporation at this time?" Guaranteed Investors Corporation had assets of only $1,000 in the bank.

The most devastating blow to the defense, it seemed to Burkett, would be to show that Taylor had a large monetary and personal interest in this project which should be considered by the jury in weighing his credibility. That was to be the prosecution's strategy.

GIC had no debts, and Taylor owned all the stock. His plan, of course, was to have the Public Employees Retirement System buy $10,000,000 in GIC promissory notes, which he would then lend out at higher interest rates. After accounting for all the fees and costs--including $25,000 to Mooney, Taylor estimated that he would personally pocket about $100,000 a year, totaling $1 million over the 10-year period.

Burkett bantered back and forth with Taylor about his memory of certain events. "When did John Rogers tell you that you could not pursue it further unless you paid him money?"

"On the 8th of November, he specifically said, 'If I help you now, you help me later'."

"Now, Mr. Taylor, in your direct testimony you said that he said that on the 4th of December, when Mr. Mooney was present with you?"

"I testified that to the best of my recollection."

"Well, you heard Mr. Finlay testify, and he didn't mention anything about Mr. Rogers saying, on the 8th of November, 'You help me and I'll help you'."

"I told you I didn't remember whether it was on the 8th or the 4th."

Taylor was further unsettled when asked, "As a matter of fact, didn't Mr. Finlay say that it was at the *end* of the conversation that Mr. Rogers said, 'My living expenses exceed my salary as Secretary of State?'" During his direct examination, Taylor graphically described the statement as having been made at the *beginning* of the meeting, almost as the first words out of Rogers' mouth. Now he wasn't sure.

"If that was his testimony," he lamely replied.

Burkett was doing everything he could to enhance the feeling among the jurors that Taylor was deliberately mocking them by his selective memory. "You testified also that on the 8th, you described to Rogers the plan and listed all of the risks involved, do you remember testifying to that?"

"Sir, I didn't have to list the risks, they were already in the offering circular."

"But that isn't my question. On direct examination, you said, 'I listed all the risks.' Now, are you changing your testimony?"

"No, sir. I am not changing my testimony."

"Then what risks did you mention to him, sir?"

"None. I gave him an offering circular, and I assumed that he read the entire offering circular."

None of this was heavyweight stuff, except that it impacted on Taylor's credibility with the jury. His testimony was fraught with that kind of loose use of the truth.

Burkett's style during direct examination was to take a yellow pad, draw a vertical line about two-thirds the way across it, and write down as nearly as he could what the witness said during direct testimony so he could read it back to him. He had been doing that for over twenty years, and the system seemed to work for him. That's what he was doing here; he had made notes of Taylor's direct examination, and he was systematically going through them.

"Mr. Taylor," Burkett explained, "I'm just trying to test your testimony. That's the purpose of cross-examination."

"I understand."

Previously, the prosecution had established through the testimony of Sara Knight that the Taylor plan was very complicated and hard to understand. Now, Burkett wanted to confirm the fact that David Hall had spent very little time evaluating the proposal before recommending it. This occurred at the December 2 meeting at Meacham field.

Burkett asked Taylor if he gave Hall any written information concerning the plan. He showed it to him, he said, but he didn't give Hall a copy.

"Did he undertake to read it?" Burkett asked.

"He looked over the information there, yes."

"Did he read it all?"

"Sir, I think he satisfied himself as to what I had represented to him."

According to Taylor, they had spent only five to fifteen minutes discussing his plan.

Burkett turned to the testimony that Mooney had accompanied Hall out to the plane when the meeting at Meacham ended. Linn had led Taylor through quite a colloquy on this during direct examination. "What conversation did you have with Mooney after he came back?" Burkett asked.

"Very little. We talked about whether we would go out to eat together or go home."

"Is that all that was said about Governor Hall?"

"Yes sir, I think he said briefly that the governor was interested in working with me on this program with other states after he got out of office or something."

"Nothing about sharing in legal fees or anything like that?"

"No sir."

"Nothing at all?" Burkett asked incredulously. Getting the truth out of Taylor was like pulling teeth.

Reluctantly, Taylor replied, "He might have mentioned legal fees when he said the governor wanted to work with me after he got out of office."

That was a significant admission. To make sure the point was not lost on the jury, Burkett asked in his most accusatory tone, "You didn't mention *that* on direct examination though, did you?" (That was more of a statement than a question.)

Taylor now looked like a man with a toothache. "Sir, the conversation didn't impress me that much to remember that much about it."

"Mr. Taylor, you heard Mr. Mooney testify about this conversation, did you not?"

"Yes sir."

"Are you telling this jury that now, today, the tenth day of March, that you don't consider that conversation to be important?"

His eyes darted back and forth, searching for an answer, any answer, that would get him out of this uncomfortable situation. "As a result of all the testimony and tapes and everything else that I've heard for two weeks, yes, but I certainly...."

"Yes, and it was important when you were testifying about it on direct examination wasn't it Mr. Taylor?"

"It was important on the fact that when he came back all he said was that they were going to try to work together after he got out of office." Taylor was now trying to alter his testimony again.

"But you didn't mention that on direct examination, why not?"

"Sir, I don't know," confessed Taylor, who was now reduced to echoing Hall who, on numerous occasions, replied, "I don't know why I said that."

Taylor had the effrontery to claim during direct examination that his plan had been "consummated" with the board. "What do you mean by that?" Burkett asked.

"That it was approved by the board," replied Taylor.

"It was unconditionally approved by the board?"

"It was approved by the board subject to the recommendation of the bank and attorney general."

"You didn't hear the testimony of the bankers that they had never recommended it?"

"They said they were not going to."

"Are you claiming that you have some contractual agreement with the Oklahoma Public Employees Retirement System at this time?"

"Objection!" roared Linn. "He's asking for legal conclusions of a lay witness."

Linn was overruled. "It's a proper cross-examination since he mentioned it on direct examination," said the judge.

Taylor was forced to answer the question. "Sir, I don't know about legally obligated, but I would think they would be morally obligated. They all voted for it.''

"Are we at a convenient stopping point?" Daugherty asked.

"Yes sir." The judge announced the noon recess.

Taylor looked relieved.

After lunch, cross-examination resumed. Taylor, back on the stand, was being caught in so many little lies that cross-examining him was almost as easy as shooting fish in a barrel.

"Did you talk to Mr. Hall between the visit at Meacham field on December 2nd and the 14th of December when you came up for an investment committee meeting?"

"I do not believe so, sir."

Burkett made a show of going over to the prosecution table and picking up some documents. "The telephone records, Exhibit 44, show that on the 3rd of December there were four telephone calls from the governor's office to you. Do you recall what those calls were about?"

"Yes, sir," he admitted. "Since you refreshed my memory, I believe those were calls as a result of the Palo Mesa presentation, he wanted me to talk to O'Hara that day."

Burkett had shown Taylor to be a habitual liar. Now it was time to move on to more meaty matters.

What better place to begin than with the role of Kevin Mooney. How much did Kevin Mooney know about the details of the plan? Not much. Did he help prepare the document? No. Was any effort made to make him fully knowledgeable about this program. Not particularly. "Then why did you take him with you to Oklahoma City?"

"Because he was the one that made the original contact with the governor, and I figured if he was going to get a finder's fee he was obligated to go along with me."

Burkett's point was to show the jury that Mooney was not Taylor's lawyer, didn't give him legal advice, and that he was there only because he was the person making the contacts relating to the payoff. Also, he hoped it didn't pass unnoticed that Taylor let slip the fact that Mooney was going to get a finder's fee, whereas earlier he denied he had ever talked with Mooney about that.

It was fascinating to note that when Doc Taylor came to the witness stand, he carried a set of the tape transcripts with him, neatly bound in a notebook, and fully indexed. David Hall had to ask for a copy from his counsel when he was on the witness stand, but Taylor brought his with him. He would leaf from page to page as Burkett talked about the various conversations.

On December 18th, Rogers began talking with Taylor about percentages. "What if I could get this through at eight percent, what's that going to do?" Rogers asked. Did Taylor remember that conversation. Yes. "What do you think he was referring to there?" Burkett asked.

Taylor said he thought Rogers was trying to make a demand on him for money, and he tried to divert him away from that conversation.

Rogers then told Taylor that Hall told him they would split $50,000, and that he, Rogers, didn't think that was very much money for this big a deal. Taylor replied that, yes, he was very familiar with that program.

"What did you mean by that, Mr. Taylor?" Burkett wanted to know.

"I was just making conversation," Taylor stammered.

"What did you understand him to mean when he said, 'Okay. David told me on the 8-1/2 percent we would split $50,000'?"

"I didn't know what he meant by that."

"Did you ask him what he meant?"

"No, sir."

"Why didn't you?"

"Because I didn't want to get into a direct discussion with him about any fees. And I was trying not to show him that I was stunned."

Taylor was in a tight spot, and he knew it. He looked around, desperately searching for support from his attorneys, from anyone, but no help was forthcoming. The jury avoided looking at him--always a bad sign.

But Taylor's ordeal wasn't over. There was more damning evidence to be mined from this conversation with Rogers. Didn't Taylor say that he couldn't pay Rogers anything, that it would have to be disclosed in the prospectus. Yes. "What were you trying to convey to him by telling him this?"

"I was really trying to divert his attention away from this conversation."

"Well, then, you said, 'So what I'm doing is, you know, paying for something else.' Tell us, Mr. Taylor, how does that correspond with your not wanting to talk to him about not paying him anything?"

"I was trying to lead him on, or lead him away from the discussion."

That excuse didn't make any sense at all. "Telling him you're going to pay for something else is leading away from the discussion about payments, is that what you want this jury to believe?"

"Yes, sir," he said weakly.

Still more. "Mr. Taylor, did you tell Mr. Rogers that it is a normal routine for you to pay people for finding money?"

"I told him it was normal for me to pay people for services rendered."

It got progressively worse rather than better. Rogers told Taylor that Hall said the deal was going to be all cash, and he couldn't see how Taylor could do that. Taylor assured him, "This is a normal routine...a standard practice to do that," indicating that cash wouldn't be a problem.

"And did you say, 'So what we do is pay for something else, okay. We look at... a half percent on ten years is worth an eighth of a point to us, okay?' What were you telling him there, Mr. Taylor?"

"Double talk."

"Sir?"

"Double talk."

Now a crunch question: "Did you intend that he feel that you would compensate him in some way for his part in this matter?''

"I was trying to make it clear to him that I would not compensate him as a direct result of this. But I was trying to lead him on that I might be willing to do something else."

"And did you say, '...and this could be a beginning relationship?'''

"My feeling at the time was, he was chairman of the investment committee, and this could be a beginning of a relationship between myself and the fund if we got it properly put together."

"Then did you say, 'After we develop a paying record, then we can lower the secure ladder a little bit and raise the rate or leave more room, you know, for the players?'''

"Yes, sir."

"You were trying to convey to Mr. Rogers, were you not, the idea that you were willing to compensate him for his assistance in this matter, is that not true, Mr. Taylor."

Taylor retreated to the same shop-worn excuse he'd tried before, "I was trying to divert him away from cash demands into future banks that would never happen."

Then he made a damning admission, "And I admit that I'd hoped that he would extract from this that it meant more for him."

It was pretty much a downhill sled-ride after that. All that remained was to drive a few more nails in the coffin.

Burkett reminded Taylor about the conversation with John Rogers on December 30th when he was called out of a meeting at First National Bank in Dallas. He said he remembered it. Taylor had asked Rogers if he was in his office; Rogers said no, that he was at his girlfriend's house, and Taylor replied, "What I mean is, can you talk?"

"Why did you ask him that?" Burkett asked.

Taylor resumed his former style, saying anything he thought might get him off the hook. "Because he opened the conversation by saying that the deal is all approved, bring the $31,250 and you

can have the commitment. I wanted... to get sufficient information
to go back to the governor and tell him exactly what Mr. Rogers
was doing.''

Burkett bore down. ''Mr. Taylor, I suggest to you that at the
time you had this conversation where you asked, 'Are you in your
office now?' and he said no, he was at his girlfriend's house, *no*
sum of money had been mentioned. Is your recollection
different?''

''Then it comes very shortly after that.''

''Yes, sir. Very shortly after that! But it hadn't been mentioned
at that time.''

Taylor had the transcript open in front of him. Burkett walked
him through it word for word.

Rogers: ''But I'm not going to give you that letter until you
bring what you're supposed to bring.''

Taylor: ''I understand.''

R: ''Now, it's eight and a quarter, so I want to know how much
it is.''

T: ''Well, you're the doctor. I thought that was for the eight
percent.''

R: (Laughter.) ''You going to get chintzy?''

T: ''No. No. Absolutely not.''

R: (Laughter.)

T: ''That's what I'm telling you. You tell me.''

R: ''Well, is that okay?''

T: ''Yeah. Let me write it down so I won't forget it.''

R: ''Okay.''

T: ''Tell me again.''

R: ''$31,250.''

T: ''And that can be given to David?''

R: ''Why sure.''

T: ''Okay. But what....''

R: ''And that's half, baby.''

T: ''But what I'm really going to do is give, uh, give it to,
uh...''

R: ''Mooney, probably.''

T: "Yeah, right."

R: "You're going to give it to Mooney. And he's going to give it to David. Right?"

T: "Right."

R: "Okay. But now that's just half, Doc. That's your first half, and when I get the ten million paid to you, you have to come up with the other."

T: "Alright, and how much is, half of what now? What...."

R: "That's 62,500."

T: "...what's my total? Pardon me?

R: "That's half of 62,500."

T: "Okay."

R: "You got people around you or something?"

T: "Well, from the numbers standpoint."

R: (Laughter.)

T: "You know."

R: "From the numbers standpoint?"

T: "Yeah."

R: (Laughter.) Okay, okay, $31,250 is one-half of $62,500."

T: "Alright, but are you, are you sharing that with somebody else?"

R: "Well, yeah, David, uh, is going to get half of his now."

T: "In other words, he gets half of what you get?"

R: "Well, you're going to give him the 31 thou... or give Mooney $31,250."

T: "Right."

R: "Mooney gives it to David."

T: "Right."

R: "$31,250."

T: "Right. I got ya."

R: "David gives half of that to me."

T: "I got ya."

R: "Okay?"

T: "I got ya."

R: "But then you owe another half."

T: "I got that."

R: "And I ain't sure where I want you to give that, 'cause David's going to be out of office."

T: "Okay."

Try as he might, Taylor couldn't wriggle off that hook. At length, he said simply, "I lied." But even that proved to be a lie, for as soon as he got back to his office Taylor had his secretary write a check to Kevin Mooney for $31,250 and mark it for legal services.

A recess was had. While the jury filed out, Burkett moved from the podium back to the prosecution table to review his notes and confer with his colleagues about what questions still needed to be asked. There was one important area yet to cover.

The jury returned. Taylor resumed the stand. Burkett resumed his questioning of the witness. "Mr. Taylor, do I understand your testimony correctly, that you had here a financially sound, very active plan to present to the board of trustees of the retirement system that was good for Oklahoma and that you were satisfied you could sell it if you were given a fair hearing, is that correct?"

"I was hopeful that I could sell it if I could have a fair hearing, yes, sir."

"After lunch on that day on the 18th, didn't Mr. Rogers take you to the attorney general's office?"

"Yes, sir, he did."

"He introduced you to the attorney general himself, did he not?"

"Yes, sir."

"Then to Mr. Emerson, the first assistant?"

"Yes, sir, he did."

"Then what did Mr. Rogers do?"

"He left."

"How long were you there in the attorney general's office, Mr. Taylor?"

"I believe for 45 minutes to an hour, maybe."

Then came another crunch question: "At any time while you were there, did you say to the attorney general, or anybody in his office, 'I'm being shaken down for a $50,000 payoff?' Did you complain that something illegal was going on in connection with your beautiful plan, which was good for Oklahoma and didn't need any payoff to sell it? Did you?''

"No, sir."

Burkett then took him through the remaining conversations, including the one on December 31 when Mooney reported that Hall told him that Rogers was trying to set him up; on January 9 when he showed Mooney the $31,250 check; on January 11 when he told Hall that Rogers had made a cash demand on him; and on January 13 when he assured Rogers he would do everything he had agreed to do.

"No further questions, Your Honor."

The judge called the attorneys to the bench. He wanted to know how much longer they thought they needed for this witness. D. C. Thomas said, "I think I can get through with this witness in 10 minutes." Jimmy Linn, whom Burkett thought would try to rehabilitate his witness, surprised them by saying, "I have no redirect."

"Are you through with cross?" the judge asked Burkett.

"Yes, sir."

Judge Daugherty took a moment to address the jury: "Ladies and Gentlemen of the Jury, by running over a little bit, we may be able to finish today, so in my discretion I'm going to ask you to bear with us a little bit longer today. You will now hear further cross examination."

D. C. Thomas rose to defend his client, David Hall. As always, he was supremely courteous. He started into the details of Taylor's arrest in Jackson, Mississippi. The prosecution objected and was overruled. Nonetheless, the judge said, "I will tell you, Ladies and Gentlemen of the Jury, I don't think it's got much relevancy as to the question of whether or not the defendants on trial are guilty or innocent of the charges against them." Thomas got off that line.

Thomas then ran through a litany of questions designed to put distance between his client and Doc Taylor.

"Mr. Taylor, Governor Hall knew nothing in the world about your telling the secretary to write a check for $31,250, did he?"

Burkett bounced to his feet. "We object to that as calling for hearsay or conclusion of this witness."

"Overruled."

"You may answer the question," Thomas prompted him.

"Yes, sir. The Governor had no knowledge of it from me. And to the best of my knowledge, he didn't know anything about it."

"Did Governor Hall, to the best of your knowledge, know anything about changing the check stub?"

"No sir. He would have no occasion to know anything about that."

"To you, or in your presence, Mr. Taylor, did Governor Hall ever discuss or suggest or ask you for a bribe?"

"No, he did not."

"I believe you stated, as Governor Hall stated, that he could not or would not do any business dealings with yourself until he left office, is that correct?"

"That's correct, sir."

Thomas thanked him and stepped away from the podium.

"Any other questions of this witness?" inquired the judge. To a chorus of "No, sirs," he advised the witness that he could step down.

The judge held the jury in place while he called another meeting of the attorneys. "I think we need to talk some about our future schedule of time." He said to the defense lawyers, "You haven't rested yet."

"I'm going to as soon as I step down," Linn said.

"Alright, what about rebuttal?" Burkett said, "I have four, Judge."

"How long is this going to take?"

"Very short," he promised.

The judge queried D. C. Thomas, "Do you anticipate any more testimony?"

"If I knew who the rebuttal witnesses were, I could tell you."

The judge was firm. "Well, I still believe we've got to move this case along towards what looks like a possible 10:30 finishing point next morning. We've got a possibility to get the case to the jury tomorrow evening. If we have only a little bit of testimony in the morning, we have four hours of argument and approximately an hour to read the Court's instructions, so we could get it to the jury."

The lawyers resumed their places. Jimmy Linn rose to announce, "If it please the Court, Defendant Taylor rests."

Now addressing the jury, Judge Daugherty said, "You heard the testimony of Defendant Taylor and Defendant Taylor rests his case, which means that both defendants have rested their case to you, Ladies and Gentlemen of the Jury, as far as the evidence is concerned. I'm advised that there will be some rebuttal evidence on behalf of the Government, we can't tell how long. The case will probably be submitted to you first thing Wednesday morning.

"I would anticipate that you should make arrangements for Wednesday evening and any following evenings that are necessary to situate yourself that you may be sequestered or held together in the custody of the marshals and the bailiff until you reach verdicts in the case. What I'm telling you is that you need not attend to this for tomorrow evening. Probably you will need to attend to it for Wednesday morning. Okay?"

While the jurors filed out, the judge asked the lawyers to remain, this time to talk about his instructions for the jury. He provided each of them a draft of his proposed instructions, asked them to read them overnight, and said he'd take their comments at 8:30 in the morning.

...Tuesday, March 11, 1975
The Courtroom. The government called only two rebuttal witnesses--not the four announced the day before. Rebuttal witnesses are called to refute testimony given by some previous witness.

First to take the stand was Gene Blackburn, sixteen-year veteran of the Oklahoma Highway Patrol, who had been David Hall's driver and part of his security detachment during 1974. Burkett put him on to rebut the testimony of Richard Wiseman who testified in Hall's behalf that troopers watched four TV monitors that covered the governor's office, that they could see whenever the governor left his office, that they never left their stations, and on the 3rd of December he never saw Hall leave the office to go to the Blue Room.

Blackburn testified that he was frequently on the 7:00 a.m. to 3:00 p.m. shift, and that he frequently left the office to pick up checks, take reports to wherever they needed to go, gas the limousine, get some coffee, or go to the bathroom. He would even leave the building sometimes to go to the Department of Safety. He said that normally only one trooper was on duty at a time. Only when he was leaving the building or would be gone for more than 20 minutes would he notify the governor's secretary.

Richard Davis, assistant special prosecutor for the Watergate Special Prosecution Force, was the government's second rebuttal witness. Jim Peters conducted the examination. Davis testified that a private investigator named Herbert Atkins from Los Angeles had come to his office in November of 1974. Atkins told him that he was working for David Hall. He alleged that Hall had been unfairly and improperly under investigation for four years, that it was an IRS investigation, and that he alleged misconduct by an IRS lawyer and by the U.S. Attorney's office in connection with that investigation. Atkins furnished no documents or any data, and Davis referred him to the person in charge of abuse by the

Internal Revenue Service within the special force.

In January of 1975, Davis testified, he was contacted by telephone by Arthur Viviani, an attorney who said he would be representing Hall in connection with certain complaints about government investigations to the Watergate office. Viviani indicated to him that there was an attempt by the White House and high officials in the Department of Justice to *get* David Hall, and Viviani asked Davis to contact the people who had been in the Nixon White House who were cooperating with him to see if they knew anything about this. He mentioned specifically Chuck Colson, John Dean and Richard Kleindienst, who had been attorney general, to see if they knew of any harassment investigation. However, Davis said, his office never received any written data or documents of any kind in connection with the complaint. He testified that "there was no statement to our office that there was any current attempt to set up Governor Hall to commit a crime at the time the allegations were being made to us."

Davis said that when he read in the Washington newspapers that Hall had been indicted for events occurring in December of 1974, he called Viviani and expressed surprise. Viviani indicated that he really wasn't familiar with that aspect of it.

With that, the prosecution rested.

D. C. Thomas put on one surrebbutal witness, Herbert Atkins, the private detective mentioned in Davis's testimony. (A surrebbutal witness is one who is called to refute the testimony of a rebuttal witness.

Atkins testified that in his conversation with Richard Davis on November 11, 1974, he mentioned John Rogers and he also mentioned John Rogers to an investigator named Passaretti.

Burkett conducted the cross-examination. Atkins said he had conducted an investigation for David Hall beginning in September of 1974, and that he had accumulated some evidence which he orally turned over to the office of the special prosecutor. He said this included an arrangement with Dorothy Pike, which he thought to be peculiar. He said he first heard about John Rogers on the 8th or 9th of November, and he went to the special prosecutor's office on the 10th but had not had an opportunity to investigate the report that he got on John Rogers.

Atkins asked the special prosecutor to investigate. "I think the whole grand jury and the hiding of Dorothy Pike to me seemed to be irregular, and I brought it to their attention. I felt it was more a political case than a criminal one."

His testimony was confusing to the jury because they had never heard of Dorothy Pike, and they were completely in the dark as to what he was talking about.

Atkins said he went back to the special prosecutor on the 7th of December, saw Passaretti and a man named Horowitz, and asked them to investigate.

Burkett asked, "Did you ever, at any time, tell anyone at the special prosecutor's office that Mr. Hall was being set up in a bribe attempt by the FBI and the Attorney General of the State of Oklahoma?"

"No."

"And by the U.S. Attorney?"

"No, I said part of it. On November 8, Mr. McDivitt told me that he had just heard from Governor Hall's wife that Secretary of State Rogers was going to set up the governor in a conspiracy with Mr. Burkett and Mr. Derryberry. I understood it was probably going to be an IRS case."

That was the end of the evidence; everybody rested. Both defendants moved for acquittal. An order of acquittal by the judge is, in effect, saying that the government had not produced sufficient evidence to meet its burden, and, if believed by the jury, would not result in a conviction.

Judge Daugherty made short shrift of that argument.

It was 11:00 a.m. The court recessed for an early lunch break, with instructions to be back at 12:30.

§ § §

13

The Summation

...Tuesday, March 11, 1975

The Courtroom. Both sides had rested. The time for summing up was now at hand. In court, the government summation always goes first, then the defense, then the government's closing argument. The government gets two turns at bat and the last word, because it always bears the burden of proof. The defense never loses its presumption of innocence.

"Ladies and Gentlemen, you have heard all the evidence in the case that will be submitted to you by both sides of the case on which you will base your verdicts. Our next order of business will be for you to hear what are called the oral arguments of the attorneys."

The jurors appeared grave and sober as the judge outlined the procedures the court would follow. "You will now hear the opening argument on behalf of the government, Mr. Burkett."

Bill Burkett's strategy in the closing argument was somewhat like that of the old-time country preacher who, when asked about his three-point sermon outline, said, "I tells them what I'm going to tell them, then I tells them, then I tells them what I told them."

First, his opening statement outlined the evidence he planned to present to the jury. Second, he presented the evidence through a multitude of witnesses and documents. And third, he reviewed all of that evidence that had come in by bits and pieces--often out of sequence--and connected it up into a coordinated whole for the benefit of the jury.

He began, "You recall in my opening statement that I tried to outline my whole case, and now I'm going to try to follow that outline and see how well we did.'' All six counts in the indictment against Hall and Taylor were reviewed.

Count I was interference with commerce by threats of violence--known as the Hobbs Act--whereby Hall told Mooney he would take $100,000 for promoting Taylor's plan and Taylor agreed to pay it, which is extortion.

The second count was called the Travel Act--the use of interstate travel or transportation in aid of a racketeering enterprise.

Count III was the single phone call from David Hall in California to John Rogers in Oklahoma on December 19.

Count IV was the call from Hall in Utah to Rogers in Oklahoma on December 26.

Count V was the travel by Taylor and Mooney from Texas to Oklahoma on December 18.

Count VI was Mooney's trip from Texas to Oklahoma at Taylor's direction on January 14.

"Each of these specific acts was willfully done by the parties, not accidentally or inadvertently, to further this plan, or scheme to get this plan of Mr. Taylor's adopted by the Board and to do so by the payment of money or the promise of the payment of money.

"Doc Taylor has admitted that he offered to pay John Rogers, and that he did so intending to influence Mr. Rogers' official act. But he said, 'Oh, I didn't mean to pay it.' Isn't that like when the traffic cop stops you and you say, 'Officer, I'll give you ten bucks to let me go,' then he arrests you for attempted bribery. How far do you think you're going to get with the court by saying, 'Oh, I didn't really intend to give him the ten dollars?' No, it just doesn't work that way.

"You've heard that the Internal Revenue Service, FBI, John Rogers and Kevin Mooney, and maybe the postal inspectors are engaged in a joint conspiracy to get David Hall. And I suggest to you that a deliberate attempt is being made here to make you think that this case is really Bill Burkett against David Hall.... The whole idea is to divert your attention away from the facts of the case. This case isn't styled Bill Burkett against anybody. It's styled, 'The United States of America against David Hall, W. W. Taylor and R. Kevin Mooney.' Much as Mr. Hall would like to make it personal, he can't do it.

"Let's say something about Kevin Mooney. Kevin Mooney was up to his ears in this thing and he was caught and made a full and clean breast of it. Hall wants to make him a conspirator. But if you believe that Kevin Mooney is a conspirator in this case, you have to believe that his lawyer, a distinguished member of the Supreme Court, persuaded or allowed, deliberately, his client to plead guilty to a felony...when he didn't do it. There isn't a lawyer anywhere that can talk a client into doing that!

"Let me say something about John Rogers. Incredibly, both defendants have attacked John Rogers' credibility. They want to point a finger at John Rogers and say, "You can't believe this man, he's an inveterate liar.' Would you say the proper way to investigate this case would have been for John to say, when Doc Taylor says, 'Where are you?' 'Well, Doc, I'm over at Paul Baresel's house. I'm in his bedroom. He's with the FBI, you know. Good old Jack DeWitt is sitting here beside me running a tape recorder.' Well, that's absurd! He lied because the FBI instructed him to lie...to keep this investigation hidden.

"Who told David Hall to lie? Who told Doc Taylor to lie? They want to try John Rogers here. Well, he's not on trial.

"Let's compare Rogers' actions to the actions of Taylor and Hall when the opportunity came to make a lot of money by committing a felony. David Hall sees a chance to make money out of Doc Taylor's deal and he demands $50,000. He tells Rogers, 'this means a lot to both of us.' He said he would fire board members for not voting it if he were still governor. He said he would punish the bank if they didn't approve. He never reported this serious crime to his friend Sam Watson, head of the crime bureau, or to his friend Curtis Harris, the District Attorney of Oklahoma County.

"Mr. Taylor agreed to pay one percent to a sitting governor, a

governor then in office. He blithely tells the Secretary of State he
will pay him, but it has to be for something else, on some
feasibility study. He wrote a check for $31,250 for the purpose of
paying a bribe.

"Now, let's contrast that with John Rogers' actions. They want
to try John Rogers. When offered a bribe, he was in the attorney
general's office within ten minutes.

"Confucius said, 'To know what is right and not do it is the
worst cowardice.' Who are the cowards here. Who are the heroes
here?

"Now, the defendants' lawyers are up next. Listen to how they
explain away their clients' actions, their admitted lies, their
admitted deceit, no faithfulness to each other, certainly no
faithfulness to the law.

"I suggest to you, Ladies and Gentlemen, that the only logical,
reasonable and acceptable explanation of all their statements is
that they were involved in a conspiracy to violate the law.

"Under the circumstances, it's your duty, Ladies and Gentlemen, hard and painful as duty often is, to find them guilty as
charged."

Defense summation began with Jimmy Linn. (To even things
out, the defense lawyers argue in reverse order of the indictment.)

Like most defense lawyers, Linn considered his summation the
pinnacle of his case, the ultimate dangerous game. He was good,
really smooth, and he knew how to persuade people. He spoke
without notes.

Linn began in a traditional way, waving the flag, telling the jury
how wonderful they were, and describing how our court system
separates our country from others. "That's a heritage I'm proud
of. I have great faith in the jury system. I have great faith in
juries, because twelve ordinary people, in this country, can just
about figure out what is right."

Basically, Linn's argument was *ad hominem*--appeal to the
gallery. He wasn't able to bring any facts to refute the
overwhelming evidence against his client, particularly the damn-

ing things said on tape--which the jury all heard--nor did he try; so the only course left open to him was to make an impassioned appeal to the jury's sympathies.

This was a serious case, he said, because of what would happen to Mr. Taylor and his family and Governor Hall if they were found guilty. It was serious because it would change everyone's lives, they would be separated from their families in prison, and their civil rights would be taken away from them. "That's why the government must prove beyond a reasonable doubt, and Judge Daugherty will tell you that, prove beyond a reasonable doubt that these men are guilty."

Reasonable doubt requires proof of such a convincing character that you would be willing to rely on it unhesitatingly in the most important of your own affairs. Therefore, "you can't decide this case on some minor contradiction of evidence, some mistake that Mr. Taylor forgot, or his testimony wasn't exactly to this or just exactly that."

Linn went on, "Mr. Burkett talks about the traffic policeman you come by. Well, Mr. Burkett indicates that he doesn't understand what Mr. Taylor's defense is and what happened in this case. I'll tell you. You've got a traffic cop that comes by and is going to give you a ticket. He says, 'I'm going to give you a big ticket if you don't give me money. You give me money. I want money now. Give me money or I'm going to give you a ticket, big ticket.' Mr. Rogers was the man demanding money, not Mr. Taylor."

Maybe Taylor did break the law by leading Rogers on, Linn acknowledged, "but if he did, he didn't know it."

"Let me tell you something. If the government goes constructing crimes like that, tries to lead people into criminal acts, and does it by giving no-prosecution letters to little men like John Rogers, it's wrong. No one can make that right. No one can sell that to this jury."

Linn saved his harshest invective for John Rogers, whom he described as a "foulmouthed man who betrayed everything that ever came to him, a man who couldn't sit on the stand and look at you like a man would, a man who was in political trouble.''

Rogers pled the Fifth Amendment; Rogers was still under a continuing injunction from the SEC; Rogers traded for a no-prosecution letter for himself and his dad; Rogers lied on cue for the FBI, and so on. ''Well, I say those things to show that John Rogers might not be just the wonderful, all-American boy that Mr. Burkett is trying to make of him. I say, he's not only not an all-American boy, he's not much of a man. I say that he's not a truthful man. I say he is a devious man who has wound his web for his own personal glory, his own personal political career. I say he's not a man to be trusted.''

As for Kevin Mooney, Linn dismissed him as ''just a loser.'' He said, ''The reason why he pleaded guilty in this case was because he did a lot of selling with Rogers that he shouldn't have done, and he got scared.... No question but what Mooney was a pitiful man in many ways, a loser. A man so demeaned in his personal desires that he could not cope with them. Undisciplined man, a man weak and afraid of anything that might come to him.''

The real losers, said Linn, were the people of Oklahoma who were in the retirement fund. They were losers because they were denied the profit they could have made on Taylor's investment. ''It was a good plan. The difference between 6.6 percent, which was the best of their investments, and 10-1/2 percent fully guaranteed by the U.S. government, was a thousand dollars a day for ten years. They're the losers, they lost on the plan.''

Linn was speaking very slowly and very deliberately. ''Well, Ladies and Gentlemen, I say this to you: The judge will tell you in his charge that a man must have intent to violate the law before he can be guilty of it. The government must prove that he did it beyond a reasonable doubt. You come through with guilty verdicts on any count for my client, his life is ruined, his career is over, he's lost his civil rights. He's got a lot riding on it. Could be away from his wife, his children, his grandchildren.''

''Mr. Burkett will be happy, maybe John Rogers will become

senator, maybe everybody else will live happily ever after, I don't know.

"On the other hand, you can come back with your verdict and show what you think of a man like Mr. Rogers, a poor pitiful man like Mr. Mooney, who's to be pitied more than censored.

"I say this to you, when you go to your jury room there will be many prayers that go with you; what you do has a deep effect on many, many people.

"Thank you for your attention."

The afternoon recess was had.

The jury was very alert, particularly the foreman, as D. C. Thomas took the podium to defend his client David Hall. Some were sitting on the edge of their seats.

Thomas' style was not as flamboyant as that of Jimmy Linn, but in his own way he was equally dramatic. He called the jury's attention to the envelope that previously he had John Rogers put his initials on. "I'm going to leave that envelope there until the very end of my closing argument, then I'm going to open it up," he told them, holding the envelope up for all to see. "See, there are his initials on the front. It's still sealed." He then placed the envelope where they could keep their eyes on it throughout his talk.

Thomas likes to "de-frock" or "de-mystify" the prosecutor, so to speak, by calling the jury's attention to--then mocking--his opponent's rhetorical techniques. In this, he comes across as a wise old patriarch of his profession who has seen it all before, heard it all before, and for whom life bears no more surprises.

"If you don't have a defense, you know what you do?" he asked the jury. "You attack the prosecutor. Now, that sounds pretty logical. If they had any bribe payment to David Hall, if they could prove him guilty beyond a reasonable doubt, I guess...possibly I would attack the prosecutor.

"No, David Hall started talking about harassment. David Hall started talking about improprieties. David Hall started becoming a little bit paranoid about telephone calls and about surveillance on him four years ago. This is nothing new to David Hall. He and his good wife and family have been putting up with this for four years.''

Another jab at the prosecutor's summation: "I'll tell you something else I'm not going to do, because it's an old prosecutor's trick. I used to be a prosecutor, and an old prosecutor's trick is to say, 'I challenge Mr. Thomas to answer these; I challenge Mr. Linn to answer these points'.'' (He paused). ''And then a smart old prosecutor got hold of me one day. He said, 'Let me tell you something. Don't you let the other man spread a bunch of little old brushfires around here and you stomp them out while the forest is burning down'.''

He peered owlishly at the jury, adjusted his eyeglasses, and asserted. ''I'm not going to do that because I don't *have* to do that; because that's an old prosecutor's trick.''

Of course, when D. C. Thomas said he wasn't going to attack the prosecution, he didn't really mean it--maybe for the reason that he really didn't have a defense, after all. He strongly implied that the whole case was a political vendetta foisted on Hall by Bill Burkett and other Republicans.

''Mr. Burkett talked about Mr. Mooney and he said, 'Do you believe that ex-Supreme Court Justice McInereny would permit him to plead guilty?' You know, Mr. Burkett has conveniently, all through this trial, forgot to mention Senator Frank Keating, who is also Mr. Mooney's lawyer, who appeared right here in this court with him, who is the Republican senator who introduced the impeachment resolution against David Hall in the state Senate; and he was unsuccessful too.

''Governor Hall may have used bad judgment when he sent the state airplane to pick up Mr. Mooney and Mr. Taylor and also when he charged a personal telephone call to the state, but that's not what he was charged with.

''There was no December the 3rd meeting in the Blue Room. There couldn't have been, unless Lieutenant Wiseman, the security guard, is a bald-faced liar. Wiseman said that no such meeting took place.'' Thomas professed to be really ''shocked'' when the government put on a rebuttal witness who said he was away from his guard station five or ten or fifteen minutes at a time.

Then, in an unmistakable allusion to the assassinations of Jack Kennedy, Bobby Kennedy and Martin Luther King, Jr., Thomas hypothesized, "I can think of three good men that are dead right now, that we need so bad in these times, because somebody took five minutes off or ten minutes off or fifteen minutes off from protecting somebody else's life.

"I think David Hall was the target from 1970, election day of 1970. They said, 'Train your guns, there's the target'."

Objection, but overruled.

Thomas now began to connect the dots, attempting a coherent explanation of the bizarre facts that the jury had been listening to for two weeks--offering them up in a way that would exonerate his client.

"Do you know where the conspiracy was in my opinion? Mooney was so desperate for a job and so desperate for money, and I think Mooney put the word on Taylor because he didn't need the governor. The governor wasn't on the board; the Governor wasn't chairman of the board."

None of the four board members who testified said they felt any pressure from the governor. They voted their own conscience. If the jury is to convict Hall, they've got to believe that he pressured, cajoled, coerced that board.

How does Derryberry fit into it? Thomas had a conjecture: "You remember, I said, 'Mr. Derryberry, you were an unnamed conspirator in an indictment, were you not, in this courthouse?' He said, 'Well, yes, I was.' The next to last question I asked him was, 'Did that press release and press conditions by Mr. Burkett help you politically?' He said, 'Yes, it did.' I said, 'Were you an announced candidate for governor? 'Yes. Yes.' Against whom, I wonder?"

Question asked, question answered: "I'll tell you against whom, against the incumbent right over there. (Pointing to David Hall) That's how Derryberry fits into it!"

Ridicule is an effective tool of argumentation, and no one was better at its use than D. C. Thomas. "Can you imagine? We've seen the Keystone Cops on movies. We have seen Laurel and Hardy, where they stumble over each other and pull down shades on themselves and stumble over buckets. Isn't *this* (gesturing towards the prosecution table) a heck of a conspiracy going on here? Isn't this a real barn-burner?"

Thomas reached for the mystery envelope, made a big show of opening it, and held it up for the jury to see the printing. "November 8th. November 8th, 1974. That's what it says."

"Some of the prosecutors asked me, 'Is there going to be anything in that envelope when you open it up? Is it some sort of magic trick?' No, sir, there is no magic about it.

"I had John Rogers tell me the first time he ever met with Taylor and Mooney, and he said November 8th. And I wrote it down, put it in here and sealed it.

"What makes that date so drastically important is this: On November 8th, that day Rogers and Mr. Mooney and Mr. Taylor met for the first time, on that day Crystal Jaworsky has lunch with Randy Floyd and Randy Floyd goes to Jo Hall's house, to the Mansion, and said, 'Jo, I want to tell you that Rogers has made some sort of a deal with the U.S. Prosecutor and is going to try to put David in jail within three weeks.'

"And on November 8th, Jo Hall calls Frank McDivitt, their family lawyer, and tells him.

"And on November 8th, if you remember the testimony of Herb Atkins, McDivitt contacts him and said, 'Get to Washington, D. C. Get there this weekend and report this to Watergate.'"

He ended with a triumphal flourish: "And that's why that is so important. I think that's the critical day of this lawsuit!"

Verbosity is an occupational hazard of the defense bar, and something few lawyers can resist. Perhaps if D. C. Thomas had ended his summation at that point and sat down, he might have left some seeds of creative doubt growing in the juror's minds. However, he did not sit down. He launched into a grand literary allusion that was too far-reaching for the jury to swallow.

"Now, John Rogers used the word, 'We were trying to nail David Hall.' When he said that word, in great 'ol big letters I wrote 'nail' on my legal pad, because I remembered that the last time someone tried to nail someone, they took the man before the magistrate and he says, 'There is no evil in this man,' but the crowd had to be pleased and he was nailed. And they said, 'Now, we are through with him. We have nailed him up there on those two pieces of wood and he's dead and we won't have to worry any more.' But three days later they found out they were wrong. And for 1975 years they have been finding out they were wrong."

Thomas continued his analogy. "I remember the other man that was nailed. 'What to do about so and so, he's a murderer, we don't want him. Let him go. We want to nail this man.' There's no bribery in that man and there's no conspiracy in that man and there's no extortion in that man, and I suggest to you that not three days but fifty three days--today is the 53rd day since the indictment was handed down--that fifty three days later they are not going to be dead and through with him, with David Hall."

This may have been one time when D. C. Thomas over-reached himself. Burkett found the analogy repulsive. It was hard to imagine anyone who would feel comfortable comparing David Hall with Jesus Christ, certainly not a jury that heard some of the awful things Hall said on tape.

The prosecution always has the last word. The government's rebuttal argument is limited to responding to what the defense has argued, to set the record straight. No new information may be introduced. The burden of proof still rests with the government's prosecutor.

Burkett was momentarily embarrassed trying to find his notes to D. C. Thomas' argument. His notes on Jimmy Linn's were right in front of him, but where his notes were on Thomas, he didn't know. They had to be there on the table somewhere, but he couldn't seem to lay his hands on them. Never mind, he would be brief and focus almost entirely on Jimmy Linn's argument.

There were only four points that he thought important enough to answer.

"Mr. Linn asked who would Mr. Taylor have reported this to. He said he's up here among strangers, and I guess he thought there were not any honest officials in the state of Oklahoma. I would like to suggest that while reporting the matter to someone, while that would be desirable and appropriate, that was not Mr. Taylor's only alternative. Why didn't he just pick up his hat and briefcase and turn around and get out of this corrupt place as fast as he could? Nobody made him stay. But he could hear over a million dollars on this deal talking to him.

"Mr. Linn says we've got to prove this man's *intent*. Now, let's take a look at Mr. Taylor's actions that might lend us some assistance in determining what his intent was. He knew and said he had to hide this payment to John Rogers. He made no report of the obviously illegal activity. He talked on the phone, quote, 'Where we don't have to guard against anything.' He put 'legal services' on Mooney's check. And then he destroyed the check and changed the check stub--all very deliberate acts.

"Mr. Linn makes a serious charge. He says the government constructed a crime here, that these FBI agents ought to be out chasing murderers. What he means is, 'They ought to leave my client alone.' Let me point out to you the facts that the crime began on December 2nd and 3rd, and the FBI didn't get into this until the 9th of December. So what crime did they construct? The crime had already been committed--the conspiracy was formed, and attempts were underway to influence the board.

"The more serious argument that Mr. Linn makes is his constant hammering on ruined careers, civil rights lost, lives ended, things of this nature. Well, now, that is a blatant appeal to sympathy. And the Court will tell you, difficult though it may be, the Court doesn't tell you don't have sympathy, the Court says don't let sympathy or prejudice enter your deliberation. You've got a difficult chore. But an appeal to your sympathy is a totally improper argument to make. It's an attempt to make you take the responsibility for the consequences of these men's acts--their free and voluntary acts, I might say.

"David Hall and Doc Taylor alone are responsible for the consequences of their acts. And if this causes them and their families to suffer, they can't blame you for it."

The notion of a government conspiracy played a big role in David Hall's testimony and in D. C. Thomas' closing argument. Burkett asked the jury to listen closely to the judge's instructions, and see whether Hall's belief that there was a conspiracy against him provided him any defense in this case.

"You know, he reminds me of a nursery rhyme from Mother Goose that I used to read to my kids. It goes:

> The man in the wilderness asked of me,
> 'How many strawberries go in the sea?'
> And I answered him, as I thought good,
> 'As many red herring grow in the wood.'

"Well, a red herring has come to mean something out of place, something diverting. And you've seen the biggest red herring of all, this garbage about a conspiracy against him."

The rest of Burkett's summation focused on what it meant for the government to bear the burden of proof, which is to prove beyond a reasonable doubt. The key word is not *doubt*, but *reasonable*--not beyond *all* doubt, not beyond *possible* doubt, but beyond a reasonable doubt.

Finally, "There are a lot of people here in this courtroom who like David Hall, believe in him, don't want to believe this nightmare, who would like to blot it out. But outside this courtroom there are millions of people who are entitled to expect that their elected officials are honest. They are watching. They want to know whether the kind of sordid, appalling, disgraceful, outrageous conduct that you've seen from these two men is going to be condoned or condemned. As I say, duty is often hard. Do your duty."

A month of investigation, a month of preparation, and two weeks of testimony went into the trial. And now it was over--except for the most important part, the jury's evaluation of proof. That would start tomorrow.

Judge Daugherty advised the jurors that they should bring a small overnight bag tomorrow because once the case was submitted to them in the morning, they would be sequestered for such time as it took them to reach a verdict. He explained, "This means you will be kept together in the custody of the bailiff. Accommodations will be arranged for you at the Skirvin Plaza Hotel. You will have lodging there. You will have dinner together at the Skirvin, or some other eating place of your choice. I have no idea how long your deliberations will be."

§ § §

14

The Verdict

...Wednesday, March 12, 1975
The Courtroom.   The weatherman dealt a widespread dose of
dampness and misery to residents as showers, scattered hail, and a
few snow flurries dotted the state.

In a front-page story, the *Daily Oklahoman* reported that Doc
Taylor was being sued for $150,000 by a Brownsville, Texas, bus
manufacturing firm for allegedly not meeting a loan commitment.
Ironically, that loan from Taylor's firm, Guaranteed Investors
Corporation, was to have come from the $10 million investment
Taylor was seeking from the Oklahoma state retirement fund.

Like almost every other federal judge, and many experienced
trial lawyers, Fred Daugherty had a near-religious belief in the
wisdom of the American jury and its mystical ability to evaluate
evidence, no matter how complicated, and to reach the correct
conclusion as to guilt or innocence more than 99 percent of the
time.

At the close of a trial, the judge gives the jury the
instructions--that is, what the law is that pertains to this particular
case. The instructions receive a lot of attention from both the
judge and the attorneys, because when a case is appealed it
always has to be appealed on some error that has occurred during
the trial. The giving of improper, or failing to give proper,
instructions can be a basis for an appeal.

Both sides file their requested instructions. The judge goes over these instructions very carefully. He's not required to give an instruction in exactly the same words that the attorney requests; rather, it is sufficient to give it substantially in his own words. If the judge fails to give a requested instruction, the attorney must object and is granted an "exception," which he can then use as a basis for appeal.

"The defendants David Hall and W. W. Taylor stand charged by the indictment containing six counts which are described to you as follows:

"The defendant, David Hall, was at all times referred to herein, the duly elected, qualified and acting Governor of the State of Oklahoma....

"W. W. Taylor, is and was at all times referred to herein, President, Treasurer and Director of Guaranteed Investors Corporation, hereinafter referred to as GIC....

"That from on or about December 3, 1974, to on or about January 13, 1975, in the Western District of Oklahoma and elsewhere, the defendant Hall did knowingly, willfully, unlawfully and feloniously attempt to obstruct, delay and effect commerce, as that term is defined in Section 1951 of Title 18, United States Code, by extortion, as that term is defined in Section 1951, Title 18, United States Code, in that David Hall did attempt to wrongfully obtain property in the form of money.

"The defendants are presumed to be innocent of each count or crime against them....

"A reasonable doubt is a doubt based on reason and common sense.... Proof beyond a reasonable doubt must, therefore, be proof of such a convincing character that you would be willing to rely and act on it unhesitatingly in the most important of you own affairs.

"The fact that you may find one of the defendants guilty or not guilty of any of the counts with which he is charged, should not control your verdict with reference to any of the other counts or offenses.

"It is your duty to give separate consideration to the case of each individual defendant on trial.

"Intent and motive should never be confused. Motive is what prompts a person to act, and intent refers only to the state of mind with which the act is done. Good motive alone is never a defense where the act done is a crime, so the motive of the accused is immaterial except insofar as evidence of motive may aid in determination of state of mind or intent.

"A conspiracy is a combination of two or more persons by concerted action to accomplish some unlawful purpose, or to accomplish a lawful purpose by unlawful means.

"One may become a member of a conspiracy without full knowledge of all the details of the conspiracy.

"One who knowingly and willfully joins an existing conspiracy is charged with the same responsibility as if he had been one of the instigators of the conspiracy.

"You are instructed as a matter of law that the payment or offer of payment of money or anything of value to a public officer in the State of Oklahoma for the purpose of attempting to influence his official action is an unlawful activity under the laws of the state of Oklahoma.

"The jury is instructed that it is proper and lawful under the laws of the United States to record telephone and oral communications, where one of the parties to the communication consents to such recording.

"Certain evidence has been introduced during the trial which reveals that a witness for the Government, John Rogers, has been the subject of investigations and inquiries by various agencies of the Federal government.... This evidence was not admitted as proof tending to reflect on the credibility of the witness John Rogers, and the jury will not consider the same for this purpose. The sole reason such evidence was admitted into evidence in this case is to allow the jury...to consider whether same may have affected the voluntariness of John Rogers to the interception of oral and telephone communications to which he was a party...

"The testimony of a witness may be discredited or impeached

by showing that he previously made statements which are inconsistent with his previous testimony.

"If a witness is shown knowingly to have testified falsely concerning any material matter, you have a right to distrust such witness' testimony in other particulars, and you may reject all the testimony of that witness or give it such credibility as you may think it deserves.

"The punishment provided by law for each of the offenses charged in the indictment is a matter exclusively within the province of the Court, and is not to be considered by the jury in arriving at an impartial verdict as to guilt or innocence...

"You are the judges of the facts, the weight of the evidence, and the credibility of the witnesses.

"The verdicts of the jury in this case must be unanimous."

Judge Daugherty's instructions ran twenty-two pages. The full weight of what they were going to have to do seemed to have dawned on the jurors. Some appeared tense and anxious.

At 10:57 a.m. the jurors and alternates were sent out, but not to deliberate. Once they were gone, Judge Daugherty invited the attorneys to make any objections to the instructions as given or to suggest additional instructions. The government had none. Emmett Colvin had thirteen objections and two new instructions. The judge listened patiently to the arguments, then overruled them on the basis that either they were contrary to the law or that they were substantially contained in the instructions he had already given.

It was 11:30 a.m. when the twelve actual jurors again left the courtroom to begin deliberations. The two alternates were dismissed.

The time for lawyering was over. The long wait began.

At 3:00 p.m. the attorneys reconvened to respond to two requests from the jury. The first message read, "We are in need of a blackboard." No objections, and so ordered.

The second message from the jury foreman read, "We request

the testimony of R. Kevin Mooney. Please advise process as to whether or not we can hear some of the tapes.''

Burkett made no objection, suggesting the transcripts could either be delivered to them, or they could come back into open court and have the testimony read to them.

D. C. Thomas objected to both requests, while Jimmy Linn objected only to the testimony being read in open court.

The jury trooped back in. Preston Kelly was the foreman. The judge said, "I realize you heard this [Mooney] testimony approximately fifteen days ago.... However, to comply with your request would occupy four to five hours of open courtroom time. I therefore...decline to grant this request in hopes you may find this unnecessary.'' But then he held out a straw: "If it comes to the point that you feel this is of vital importance to you, you may renew the request and I will give it my further consideration.''

With regard to replaying the tapes, the judge said he considered the request too broad; however if they could identify any specific tape by date and participants, he "would look with more favor on the request.''

The jurors retired to continue their deliberations. At 7:30 p.m. the jury returned again to the courtroom; no verdict had been reached. The clerk collected the exhibits, the judge recessed for the evening, and the jurors were escorted to the Skirvin Plaza Hotel for the night.

...Thursday, March 13, 1975

The Fidelity Bank Plaza. The jury deliberated six hours and 15 minutes, then knocked off early at 4:30 p.m. because one of the jurors was not feeling well and might need to see a doctor.

While the jurors deliberated in the courthouse, defendants Hall and Taylor were across the street in their attorneys' offices. Normally, attorneys and defendants are asked to remain in the courthouse during deliberations, but in this case Judge Daugherty allowed them to leave. Both D. C. Thomas and Jimmy Linn had offices near each other on adjacent floors of the Fidelity Bank Plaza, just across the street south from the courthouse complex.

Publicly, David Hall continued to maintain his composure, his ebullient, jovial, confident manner. He told reporters he was feeling "good" about the outcome of the case, and he felt "encouraged" by the length of time the jury was using to decide the case. "This shows they are weighing the evidence.

"I am confident I will be vindicated. If it had been going the other way, they already would have reached a verdict," he said later in the afternoon.

Taylor, meanwhile, was giving no interviews, but he appeared outwardly confident.

Despite their outward appearances, both men shared one common bond--a vigil to wait out a verdict by the twelve jurors who were deciding their fate. If convicted on all four charges against him, Hall would face a maximum penalty of 35 years in prison and $40,000 in fines; Taylor 15 years in prison and $30,000 in fines.

Judge Daugherty's secretary called the offices at 4:15 p.m. and told the attorneys to come to court with their clients. No one knew at that time if a verdict had been reached.

Mrs. Taylor indicated the suspense was a horrifying experience for her. She said all she was doing until the jurors returned, was praying.

While leaving the federal courthouse, Hall was asked his feelings after two days of deliberations.

"Good news today," he said. "I just felt like the way the jurors looked today, it was not a convicting jury.

"They looked like they were either deadlocked, or there was an acquittal in the wind."

When informed that a vindictive legislature had filed an impeachment resolution against John Rogers, Mrs. Hall quipped, "It should have happened two months earlier!"

...Friday, March 14, 1975
Judge Daugherty's Chambers. The sun beamed on Oklahoma City through clearing skies, with temperatures in the mild 40s.

The weather outside contrasted with the mood inside. A crisis of major proportions had reared its ugly head and was threatening to undo the process. One of the jurors, Dell Meyer, had been taken to the emergency room of St. Anthony's Hospital at 5:25 that morning, fearing a possible heart attack.

Judge Daugherty asked the attorneys on both sides to consider agreeing to allow the eleven remaining jurors to continue to deliberate and reach a verdict if they could--which was permissible under federal rules.

That was fine with Burkett, and he even drafted a stipulation to that effect. But the defense was of a different mind. D. C. Thomas moved for a mistrial. Jimmy Linn joined the motion.

Judge Daugherty advised both sides that he had talked with Juror Meyer's doctor on the telephone about 10:30. The doctor said that Meyer did *not* suffer a heart attack, that she would be able to resume deliberations about 1:30, and that he had released her from the hospital for this purpose. On this professional information, the judge overruled Thomas' motion.

This precipitated another prickly exchange. Thomas asserted, "It would be my intent...to issue two subpoenas for these two physicians and on their attendance to the Court, to renew a motion for mistrial."

"Do whatever you want to do, Mr. Thomas," snapped the judge.

"All right."

"I would suggest to you, now, if you want to assist in the administration of justice, that you drop this juror and proceed with eleven."

"Well, that right has to be exercised...."

The judge was coldly furious. "You want your cake and eat it both here. I'm simply speaking now as a neutral person trying to administer justice, that I don't look with much favor on one who has a right and will not utilize it and wants to make a technical record." He added, "And I want the Circuit Court of Appeals to know this, now, how I feel about this."

Thomas was doing everything he could to get a mistrial. By now he had given up hope of an acquittal, so he didn't have

anything to gain by agreeing to excuse a juror. He protested that
he was not free to exercise a waiver without his client's full,
complete understanding.

Daugherty issued a stern lecture. "When I speak of 'you' I
speak of your client, who is also a lawyer, who knows full well
what he can do and what the administration of justice requires. In
all fairness, I simply again reiterate, I don't look with much favor
upon people who are supposed to know better, who want to have
their cake and eat it too--not exercise a valid right and let this lady
go, yet you want to take advantage of the fact that she's had to be
administered to by a doctor, which doctor says she is perfectly
ready and able to go back and resume her deliberations.

"On that basis," he concluded, "We're going to resume at
1:30."

At 2:40 p.m. the lawyers reassembled in Judge Daugherty's
chambers for the next act in this drama. Thomas moved to
reconsider his motion for a mistrial and asked to present the
testimony of the two physicians who had treated Ms. Meyer,
Doctors Richtner and Sanbar. Linn joined the motion. Burkett
raised no objection. So the judge dispatched the bailiff to go down
and knock on the jury's door, tell them to stop deliberating, and to
bring Juror Meyers back to his chambers.

"We're having a little appearance here before the court with all
the parties concerned," he apologized when she arrived. "We
regret your occurrence this morning and just want to be sure
everything is the way it ought to be. It's desired that we ask your
doctors a few questions."

"Yes."

"There is in law what's known as a *privilege* between the
doctor and the patient. Before these doctors can disclose anything,
it's necessary you agree to it. Are you willing to so agree?"

"Yes, I do."

Ms. Meyer signed the two consent forms, and the judge
instructed the bailiff to escort her back to the jury deliberation
room. "Tell the jury they may resume their deliberations when

you're there. It will be the court's order that you not divulge what has occurred at this appearance before the court."

Then they heard the two doctors. The first was Dr. Kenneth Richtner, a surgery resident at St. Anthony's Hospital, who took the original call. He examined Ms. Meyer between 5:00 and 5:30 in the morning when she complained of chest pain, but he couldn't find any evidence of a heart problem so he gave her 50 milligrams of Demerol. Richtner testified that Demerol would wear off in three to four hours and wouldn't have any effect on her thinking ability. Daugherty cross-examined him at great length to assure himself--and the record--that the medication would not adversely impact her thinking.

The second physician was Dr. S. S. Sanbar, a cardiologist, who was Ms. Meyer's regular physician. He testified that she had called him about 6:00 p.m. the evening before complaining of mild chest pains and constipation. He prescribed a sleeping pill, Dalmane, Valium and Ex-Lax. He had seen her again that morning after Dr. Richtner had treated her. He concurred that she had no heart attack. He prescribed Valium again and told her: "Now, we can keep you here for observation," but she insisted: "No, I'm okay, I'm ready to go, I feel a lot better." Dr. Sanbar emphasized the point that Ms. Meyer had voluntarily left on her own to go back to the jury room.

Burkett asked Dr. Sanbar about the fact that she had appeared in chambers and had signed these releases and apparently understood them, and did he think she had any problem with her thinking? "I have accepted the consent with the assumption that she was clear of mind," he replied.

Again, as he had done previously with Dr. Richtner, Judge Daugherty launched an extensive cross-examination. Undoubtedly, he did not wish to leave any stone unturned.

In the midst of the judge's cross-examination, a deputy came in and handed him a note.

The judge interrupted his questioning. "I might advise you gentlemen, that the jury has reached a verdict," the judge said.

Sanbar resumed his testimony. At no time did he say that Juror

Meyer was the least bit unable to function in any degree at all, but it was hard to pin him down to a clear, concise, and definite answer. With him, everything was within the realm of "could" and "possible."

The judge reminded those present that the jury had reached a verdict, but first he wanted to conclude the business at hand. "I saw no evidence to indicate that Ms. Meyers could not carry on her obligations and duties as a juror beginning at 1:30 today."

Turning to the defense, and to D. C. Thomas in particular, he asked, "Do you want to move for mistrial?"

Thomas conferred with his client, David Hall, then renewed his request for a mistrial, claiming error on Judge Daugherty's part in allowing the jury to go back to work at 1:30. Linn joined the motion.

Daugherty carefully recited the facts for the record, then made his ruling: "After having heard the doctors and having seen her and conversed with her, your motions for a mistrial will be overruled."

The Courtroom.   At 4:40 p.m. the participants in this drama returned to their places: the jury in its box, the judge on his bench, the lawyers and defendants at their tables, and the press and spectators in their pews. The trial was now ready to enter its final phase--the announcement of a verdict.

The lawyers scanned the jurors' faces, seeking to discern some clue as to how they voted. The jurors remained passive, inscrutable.

Linn and Taylor leaned forward in their chairs, their arms on the defense table. They were solemn.

Thomas leaned back in a swivel chair, and Hall sat erect with a half-smile. Both seemed confident.

The entire court seemed collectively to hold its breath as Judge Daugherty asked:

"Mr. Foreman, has the jury reached a verdict in the case?"

Foreman Preston Keely rose. "We have, Your Honor."

"Would you please hand the verdicts and the other papers to

the bailiff?'' It was done, and the bailiff, in turn, delivered the papers to the court clerk who handed the verdicts to the judge.

Judge Daugherty read them and handed them back to the clerk. As soon as he was satisfied that the clerk had the papers in their proper order, the judge intoned, "The clerk will read the verdicts.''

"We, the jury, find the defendant, David Hall, guilty as charged in Count One of the indictment. Signed March 14, 1975. Preston R. Kelly."

A gasp swept across the courtroom. A governor of their state had been found guilty of a crime which he committed while in that high office. David Hall remained expressionless. The shoulders of Jo Hall, sitting next to Mrs. Taylor, jerked involuntarily, then stiffened. Both women stared straight ahead.

The same litany was repeated for each of four verdicts against David Hall and three verdicts against W. W. Taylor.

"Are these the verdicts of each and every member of the jury? If not, it's your duty to speak up and let me hear you at this time.''

Silence.

"Hearing nothing, the Court assumes that these are the unanimous verdicts of each member of the jury.''

After a brief conference with the lawyers, during which it was determined that there was no more business, the judge thanked the jury for performing an important civic responsibility.

"Now, if there is nothing further, Ladies and Gentlemen of the Jury, you are discharged.''

To the defendants, Judge Daugherty advised that sentencing would be set for a later date. They needed to report to a United States Probation Officer for preparation of a pre-sentencing report. And in the meantime, they might remain at liberty under their present bonds.

After leaving the hushed courtroom, Hall said he was "surprised" by the verdict but maintained his composure and held his usual confident manner. He called the trial only "round one" and a "temporary defeat."

Taylor was visibly shaken by the verdicts and still professed his innocence as he left the courthouse. When asked what he was thinking as the verdicts were read, Taylor said, "Nothing."

"What are you going to do now?" he was asked.

"We're still innocent," was his response.

"That's right," added Mrs. Taylor, holding back tears.

Mrs. Hall would not comment on the verdicts.

"This completes round one," Hall said. "I've directed my attorney to file for a new trial and to appeal the verdict in this case.

"I was very much surprised. I expected a verdict of not guilty on each count, or I expected a hung jury," he said.

§ § §

15

Epilogue

...Friday, April 25, 1975

The Courtroom.

"Each of you has appeared before the Court, you entered pleas of not guilty to the charges against you, you were afforded a trial by jury. The jury returned its verdicts, verdicts of guilty as to each of the counts with which you were charged.... I am now ready to pronounce sentence....

"Before doing so, the court invites each defendant to make any statement you wish to make to the court... in mitigation of punishment."

DEFENDANT HALL: "Your Honor, not withstanding the verdict of the jury, I stand before the Court this morning and I state to the Court that I am not guilty of these charges...."

THE COURT: "Defendant Taylor?"

DEFENDANT TAYLOR: "I leave it in your hands, Judge."

MR. LINN: "I say this on behalf of my client: he's not a man who belongs in prison nor would it serve any purpose for him to be there, in my opinion."

MR. COLVIN: "Being a resident of Dallas, which is the same residence of Mr. Taylor, I have come to know Mr. Taylor very well. I find that his character and reputation is impeccable."

COURT: "It will be the judgment and the sentence of the Court that Defendant Hall... is sentenced to the custody of the Attorney General...for a period of three years.

"It is the judgment and sentence of the Court that Defendant

Taylor... is ordered sentenced to the custody of the Attorney General for a period of eighteen months.''

Both defendants appealed. On May 11, 1976, the 10th Circuit rejected their appeal in a unanamous 33-page opinion. The U.S. Supreme Court refused to hear their case.

Hall began serving his sentence at Swift Trails Federal Prison near Safford, Arizona. After serving eighteen months he was paroled in May, 1978. He and his family then moved to San Diego, California, where he engaged in a succession of mostly failed business ventures. In January 1983, Hall and his wife settled with the Internal Revenue Service for $325,000 for the federal income tax claim covering the period when he served as governor.

Apparently old habits die hard. Hall's name popped up in the news again in May 1995 when he was terminated as chairman of the San Diego Senior Sports Festival for having driven that organization's debts to an excessive level.

The authors have no current information on the whereabouts of W. W. Taylor.

William R. Burkett left the U.S. Attorney's office on September 1, 1975, to join the law firm of Linn, Helms, Kirk and Burkett. In March 1987, he was appointed District Judge for Oklahoma County.

Burkett left the bench in August 1988 to join the law firm of Hall, Estill, Hardwick, Gable, Golden and Nelson which has offices in Tulsa, Oklahoma City, and Washington D.C.

In June 1989, he was appointed by Governor Bellmon as chairman of the state Human Services Commission, an office he held until July 1, 1992. He again served as District Judge from January 1997 to January 1999.

Mr. Burkett continues to practice law as general counsel for the Oklahoma Corporation Commission.

§ § §

Chapter Notes

Chapter 1.

1. Some time after the fact, Burkett recalled having signed a letter at the request of the IRS to Oklahoma County District Attorney Curtis Harris asking him to withdraw a grand jury subpoena for Dorothy Pike, saying that the IRS was providing her "protective services."

Chapter 2.

1. Tulsa attorney Frank M. Hagedorn reported that he received a call from two IRS agents advising him that Dorothy Pike was in Missouri and would be calling him. Ms. Pike said that she was in fear of her life. Hagedorn drove her by car to Jackson, Mississippi, changed her name, changed her hair style and color, got her a job, and concealed her for nearly a year. The IRS never knew where she was, nor did they want to know. From time to time, however, they would make arrangements through Hagedorn to meet her some place, usually on the east or west coast.

Chapter 3.

1. *Daily Oklahoman*, March 12, 1974, story by Mike Hammer, p. 1, copyright 1974 Oklahoma Publishing Company.

2. On Thursday, September 12, 1974, the Circuit Court of Appeals, Denver, heard arguments on the matter of the disbarment. The panel consisted of Judges Jean S. Breitenstein, presiding, James E. Barrett and William E. Doyle. Neil Koslowe, an attorney from the Department of Justice, argued for the disbarred attorneys; and Walter A. Steele, a Denver lawyer appointed by the Circuit, argued for Chandler. Mr. Steele argued

that Judge Chandler's actions were not final, and that the matter should be sent back to him where Burkett and his colleagues would be allowed to defend themselves. Mr. Koslowe argued that Judge Chandler had already disbarred them without giving them an opportunity to be heard, and the case should be thrown out without any further proceedings.

On November 11, the Circuit Court ruled that the disbarments were void because they were not supported by the evidence. The opinion, written by Judge Doyle, said: "...we find no evidence establishing contemptuous refusal to obey specific orders and find no evidence that Burkett misled the court or failed in any obligation to serve the court." The opinion found for all six attorneys in every respect and concluded with the words, "We merely say that the dearth of evidence in support of [Judge Chandler's] adjudications is so plain that the accused attorneys are not to be subjected to meaningless procedure in connection with these contempt citations."

Steven Chandler petitioned the court for a rehearing. It was denied. He then asked the Supreme Court to hear the case. That petition was denied on October 6, 1975.

3. It was reported to the Author in 1993 that prior to entering his disbarment order, Judge Chandler had consulted Granville Tomerlin, a highly regarded lawyer in Oklahoma City, about the matter. Tomerlin told him he would have to give them notice and have one of the other judges hear the matter. Chandler's response was, "Why, none of them would disbar them!"

4. *Daily Oklahoman*, Wednesday, March 13, 1974, AP story by Tom Laceki, p. 12, copyright 1974 Oklahoma Publishing Co.

5. In an opinion handed down June 7, 1974, the Circuit Court stated, "...the action of the District Court has been and is now without jurisdiction in that the suit would seek to enjoin the defendants, petitioners here, from pursuing official duties. Thus it is outside the jurisdiction of the District Court."

Chapter 4.

1. *Daily Oklahoman*, April 25, 1974, p. 1.

2. *Daily Oklahoman*, May 16, 1974, p. 1.

3. *Daily Oklahoman*, April 25, 1974, p. 1.

4. Copies of the fraudulent letters were supplied to Burkett.

5. *Daily Oklahoman*, April 25, 1974, p. 1.

Chapter 5.

1. The original amount requested was $20 million, later scaled back to $10 million.

2. A "point" means one percentage point, or, in this case, $100,000.

3. Previously, Burkett had prosecuted Leo Winters, charging that he had a deal whereby for a kickback of $250.00 per month for each $1 million deposited, he would deposit state funds in a bank, interest free. Since the state had many millions on deposit at any given time, receiving interest-free deposits was to a bank like "finding money in the street."

Chapter 7.

1. After Bill Burkett left the U.S. Attorney's office in the late summer of 1975, Jimmy Linn asked him to join his law firm, which became Linn, Helms, Kirk & Burkett. Mac Oyler, who handled Hall's appeal, filed a copy of the announcement with the 10th Circuit Court of Appeals. W. W. Taylor was quoted as "having serious doubts about Jimmy Linn's defense."

2. *Voir dire*--"to speak the truth"--relates to the questioning of prospective jurors about their competence to render a fair and impartial verdict.

3. Twelve cities in the Western District are designated as *court towns,* such as Guymon, Woodward, Enid, Lawton, Mangum, etc. If a determination is made that the defendant cannot get a fair trial in the town where the court is sitting, the court can change venue to one of these other towns.

4. In criminal court, the defense does not have access to "discovery" in the same the way they do in civil court. There are no surprises in a civil action--or at least there shouldn't be--because both sides have a chance to depose all witnesses and

see all the exhibits. Nevertheless, as U.S. Attorney, Burkett followed an "open file" policy and routinely showed the defense everything he had.

5. A government wiretap order is not easy to get. Understandably, the rules for maintaining the Fourth Amendment protections are very strict. Before applying to a court for a wiretap authorization, the government must demonstrate a good-faith basis to believe that illegal activities will be overheard. It also must demonstrate a continuing good-faith effort not to listen to other kinds of conversations on the same line, such as chats with wives, doctors, girlfriends, and legitimate business calls. If agents fail to obey the rules, the judge can suppress the tapes.

6. The *record* refers to the product of the court reporter, who takes down every word uttered in the courtroom by the judge, lawyers and witnesses, together with the exhibits that are offered. If there is an appeal, the appellate court sees only the record and may not consider anything that is not in the record. Therefore, it is extremely important to both sides that their objections be in the record.

Chapter 11.

1. Burkett learned later that the reason D. C. Thomas' opening statement was so short was because David Hall had never given him any kind of a coherent story that would explain the facts, why he would say some of the things he said on tape, or why W. W. Taylor would say some of the things he said on tape.

2. Curtis Harris was the District Attorney for Oklahoma County.

Index of Names

ABOUT THE AUTHORS

William R. Burkett, an attorney in Oklahoma City, received his LL.B. and J.D. from the University of Oklahoma Law School. He has been a State Representative, U.S. Attorney, District Judge, and Presiding Judge of the Oklahoma Temporary Court of Appeals.

James Edwin Alexander is former dean of the Meinders School of Business at Oklahoma City University. He received his education from the University of the Pacific, Boston University, Claremont Graduate School, and Vanderbilt University, earning a Ph.D at the latter institution. The author of 19 previous books, he is listed in *Who's Who in the World* and *Who's Who in Finance and Industry*.

Cover design: Larry White
Copy editing: Katherine Yates